HISTORICAL
INVESTIGATION
and
NEW TESTAMENT
FAITH

HISTORICAL
INVESTIGATION
and
NEW TESTAMENT
FAITH

Two Essays

FERDINAND HAHN

Translated by Robert Maddox

Edited and with a Foreword by Edgar Krentz

FORTRESS PRESS　　　　PHILADELPHIA

The first essay is a translation of "Probleme historischer Kritik,"
Zeitschrift für die neutestamentliche Wissenschaft 63 (1972): 1–17,
copyright © 1972 by Ferdinand Hahn.

The second essay is a translation of "Methodologische Überlegungen
zur Rückfrage nach Jesus," in *Rückfrage nach Jesus. Zur Methodik
und Bedeutung der Frage nach dem historischen Jesus*, 2d. ed. Edited
by Karl Kertelge. Quaestiones Disputate 63. Freiburg: Herder, 1974,
pp. 11–77. Copyright © 1974 by Verlag Herder KG Freiburg im
Breisgau.

Library of Congress Cataloging in Publication Data

Hahn, Ferdinand, 1926–
    Historical investigation and New Testament faith.

    Translation of: Probleme historischer Kritik and
Methodologische Überlegungen zur Rückfrage nach Jesus.
    Includes bibliographical references and index.
    Contents: Problems of historical criticism — Method-
ological reflections on the historical investigation
of Jesus.
    1. Bible. N.T. — Criticism, interpretation, etc. —
Addresses, essays, lectures. 2. Jesus Christ —
Historicity — Addresses, essays, lectures. I. Krentz,
Edgar. II. Hahn, Ferdinand, 1926– . Probleme
historischer Kritik. English. 1983. III. Hahn,
Ferdinand, 1926– . Methodologische Überlegungen zur
Rückfrage nach Jesus. English. 1983. IV. Title.
BS2361.2.H33. 1983   220.6'7'01   82–48547
ISBN 0–8006–1691–X

9759A83   Printed in the United States of America   1–1691

CONTENTS

ABBREVIATIONS

ASNU	Acta seminarii neotestamentici upsaliensis
BEvTh	Beiträge zur evangelischen Theologie
BZ	*Biblische Zeitschrift*
n.s.	new series
BZNW	Beihefte zur *Zeitschrift für die neutestamentliche Wissenschaft*
ConNT	*Coniectanea neotestamentica*
ET	English Translation
EvTh	*Evangelische Theologie*
Facet Books, BS	Facet Books, Biblical Series
Forsch.z.syst.u. ökumen.Theol	Forschungen zur systematische und ökumenische Theologie
FRLANT	Forschungen zur Religion und Literatur des Alten und Neuen Testaments
Herm. Unters. z. Theol.	Hermeneutische Untersuchungen zur Theologie
JBL	*Journal of Biblical Literature*
NTS	*New Testament Studies*
QuDisp	Quaestiones Disputatae
RGG	*Religion in Geschichte und Gegenwart*
Samml. gemeinverständl. Vortr.	Sammlung gemeinverständlicher Vorträge
SBS	Stuttgarter Bibelstudien
SBT	Studies in Biblical Theology
StTh	*Studia theologica*
ThB	Theologische Bücherei

ThLZ	*Theologische Literaturzeitung*
ThQ	*Theologische Quartalschrift*
ThR	*Theologische Rundschau*
TRev	*Theologische Revue*
TThZ	*Trierer theologische Zeitschrift*
VF	*Verkündigung und Forschung*
WMANT	Wissenschaftliche Monographien zum Alten und Neuen Testament
WUNT	Wissenschaftliche Untersuchungen zum Neuen Testament
ZNW	*Zeitschrift für die neutestamentliche Wissenschaft*
ZThK	*Zeitschrift für Theologie und Kirche*

FOREWORD

BIBLICAL INTERPRETATION is an indispensable activity of the church, through which the church draws on Scripture for its proclamation, its worship, its mission, and its confession. It is also a technical, academic activity practiced by professional interpreters in college, seminary, and university. In both communities there is currently unrest over the historical-critical method, the regnant scholarly method of recent decades.

That unrest is not confined to church over against academy, or American over against European scholarship, or conservative evangelical Christianity over against the older (and more open) Protestant denominations. It can be found in differing degrees everywhere. It may divide scholars within the same denomination,[1] or be expressed by a representative of evangelical Christianity over against other Christians as a *Battle for the Bible*,[2] or be expressed by scholars who continue to practice historical criticism while calling either for other methods[3] or for a fundamental discussion of the historical and theological validity of historical criticism.

In Germany that call has come primarily from Peter Stuhlmacher and Ferdinand Hahn. These two scholars agree that historical criticism is in need of a thorough evaluation. Stuhlmacher[4] speaks of the situation of contemporary New Testament studies as a Miserere, a crisis situation; he suggests that critical study of the Bible be seen as part of a larger task—study of the tradition of acceptance and interpretation of the Scriptures in the church (*Wirkungsgeschichte*).[5]

The present volume makes available to American scholarship and the church two contributions by Ferdinand Hahn.[6] The first (and shorter) essay addresses specifically the problems that come with

9

the historical-critical method's origins in positivist history. Hahn is concerned especially with the estrangement, the alienation, that critical study brings to the biblical texts — which is contrary to the intention of these texts. That estrangement is the result of a too narrow mode of thought that isolates biblical texts from all transcendent points of reference. Thus historical-critical interpretation pushes biblical texts into the past — which is contrary to the message of the New Testament that speaks to the present and opens the future. The first essay ends with an almost passionate plea for the recognition of these problems and a call to join in the search for a solution.

The second (far longer) essay, written less than two years later, makes major contributions to the solution through a consideration of the preeminent historical question posed in New Testament scholarship during the last two centuries — the quest for the historical Jesus. Here the first two parts of the discussion delineate the nature of the problem and the resources available for studying the historical Jesus. While Hahn here traverses ground that is familiar to New Testament scholarship, he does so with the evident intention of raising at each step the historical problematics and contributions of the quest. His discussion of criteriology for the quest is an impressive contribution to the ongoing debate. He concludes that historical skepticism is in no way justified.

In the final part of this second essay Hahn turns to the historical and theological problematics of the quest as an example of critical historical thinking in order to discuss the relevance and theological justification of such thinking. Here he argues that one should not draw a false boundary between the earthly Jesus and the risen and exalted Lord. The historical approach, legitimate to be sure, requires a theological validation. Hahn finds this validation in the story of the early church's "reception" of Jesus. He also points out the dangers of a purely historical approach, for there are dogmatic implications in such a hermeneutic. The challenge is to use historical investigation for illuminating the way in which the Jesus tradition was taken into the kerygma. This would aid in overcoming the positivism of historical criticism. Detailed academic research must be supplemented by good intuition about the historical significance of Jesus. Ultimately, says Hahn, understanding of the pre-Easter Jesus depends on being grasped in faith by this Jesus, who is both the Christ and the living word. Scholarship and faith are not antithetical but complementary, and both are necessary for understanding.

Hahn's distinctive contribution is this strong demand — made by a scholar informed by faith — for rigorous historical investigation within the context of the history of the Jesus tradition in the church. Hahn poses for American scholarship the theological question of the relation between method and faith. It is in the posing of that question that Hahn's book will make its major contribution to the American discussion of biblical interpretation.

NOTES

1. See, for example, *Studies in Lutheran Hermeneutics*, ed. John Reumann (Philadelphia: Fortress Press, 1979), pp. 269–367.
2. So Harold Lindsell, *The Battle for the Bible* (Grand Rapids: Zondervan, 1976).
3. See, for example, Walter Wink, *The Bible in Human Transformation* (Philadelphia: Fortress Press, 1973). He calls for a communal, meditative approach, under psychoanalytical guidance, along with continued use of historical methods.
4. See Peter Stuhlmacher, "Thesen zur Methodologie gegenwärtiger Exegese," *Schriftauslegung auf dem Wege zur biblischen Theologie* (Göttingen: Vandenhoeck & Ruprecht, 1975), p. 61; his essay was originally a companion piece to the first essay in this Hahn volume.
5. See Peter Stuhlmacher, "Neues Testament und Hermeneutik," *Schriftauslegung*, pp. 35ff.
6. Hahn's career and bibliography have been surveyed by John Reumann in Ferdinand Hahn, *The Worship of the Early Church* (Philadelphia: Fortress Press, 1973), pp. v–xix.

PROBLEMS OF
HISTORICAL CRITICISM

TODAY IN MANY QUARTERS it is alleged that the accepted ways in which scholars pose their questions are inadequate. Frequently this allegation is associated with the charge that academic research is ineffective in meeting the demands of contemporary praxis. Insofar as this charge is only intended to prove the need for a "critical theory," of whatever kind, the question must arise whether such a concept of method does justice at all to the biblical texts. But there can be no doubt that it is essential to review the theoretical approach taken in scholarly work from time to time; and certainly problems have arisen in exegesis precisely because the discussion of methodology has not been carried through with enough autonomy and intensity.

In biblical research, the problem of method has its focus in the use of historical criticism. In Protestant circles, and increasingly in Catholic circles as well, the validity and necessity of historical criticism for the interpretation of the Old and New Testaments is taken for granted. It is described and applied in a way that corresponds with the principles of historical and literary studies in general. In addition, it is connected (often by a quite tenuous thread) with a particular theological frame of reference, though the latter does not affect the method itself. This frame of reference has as its purpose simply to allow the historical-critical method enough room to move within exegesis.[1] But it is precisely because the method is as a rule applied in so unreflective a way that exegetical work is weighed down and in countless instances baffled. The hermeneutic discussion, carried on intensively over the past three decades, has been unable to prevent this, because something has obviously gone wrong in the practice of historical-critical

13

exegesis itself, so that our difficulty at the moment is not so much with unresolved hermeneutic problems as with unresolved problems of exegetical method.[2] Hence discussion must be directed to this sensitive point, if we wish to make progress.[3]

But the significance of the hermeneutic endeavors of the recent past should by no means be overlooked. For the very point of these endeavors was to emphasize both the indispensability and the theological legitimacy of the historical-critical method in biblical scholarship. The view was held, not without substantial reason, that the systematic application of historical criticism corresponds to the Reformers' conception of justification by faith alone, because one relinquishes any security through external facts and ecclesiastical tradition, and appeals only to the kerygma, over which one exercises no control; and one will not easily be able to exaggerate the importance of this concept.[4] But the existentialist interpretation associated with this hermeneutic proposal no longer has the same integrative power today that it had a few years ago; it is no longer able to open up the understanding of biblical texts on the basis of contemporary thought, and at the same time to overcome the historical problems in this process of understanding. The discrepancy between historical and theological interpretation is therefore once again being felt much more strongly, and it is of critical importance not to let this tension become intolerable. But that is possible only if we apply ourselves to the problems of historical criticism, which are coming more and more clearly into view.

I

It is impossible to give an outline of the history of theology as it bears on the question before us, so as to explain how historical-critical exegesis has been used and what difficulties have been associated with it.[5] Nevertheless, let us highlight a few typical instances, because this will help us appreciate the present situation.

It ought not be disputed that we find ourselves at the end, or in a late phase, of a process of disintegration that has been going on for several centuries. That need not be a negative judgment from the start; it is simply a matter of stating a fact. It must also be affirmed that we are today experiencing the momentum of this process of disintegration to a special degree.

For the period of the Reformation, historical and theological explanation of Scripture did not coexist in tension-laden proximity. The *sensus literalis*, as distinct from all attempts by a human tradition to interpret the text, was willy-nilly the *sensus propheticus*. But the true meaning of Scripture was also the meaning applicable to the present time, and a distinction between the time of the early church and one's own time was not felt in the matter of intellectual context. A stronger historical differentiation may on the other hand have been entirely necessary; and a distinction between the *sensus literalis* and the *sensus propheticus* may have turned out to be unavoidable. But the decisive factor at that time was precisely the convergence of both perspectives, which for us, in view of modern presuppositions of thought and research, is in danger of being completely lost to view; and that often leads to a polarization in which the two have no connection at all.

Yet the fact should not be overlooked that the first impulses toward historical criticism go right back to the fifteenth and sixteenth centuries, and are part and parcel of the humanistic principle of returning to the sources. This was the means by which unjustified claims on behalf of tradition were to be exposed and broken through, and the original and true understanding of a matter was to be brought back into the light. Up until that time, a historical phenomenon has always been seen in indissoluble and ultimately unproblematic fusion with the history of its effects. The authoritative understanding of a phenomenon was the one which the history of interpretation transmitted, which had come into effect at some point of time and had come down to the present. Thus the understanding of history depended on an interpretation that came to prevail later on, and that was by no means necessarily identical with the beginnings of the understanding of the historical matter in question. On the other hand, the unity between a historical datum and a subsequent process of understanding was thereby assured; or, to put it more precisely, there was a firm tradition of understanding, which was essentially uncontested. Of course, that does not mean that there were no difficulties of understanding and no disputes about the interpretation of historical facts in that era; but in principle the historical question and the question of interpretation coincided. At first that was not basically changed by humanism and the Reformation, because their concern was with the original and therefore true understanding of historical facts, over against any and every secondary interpretation of them.

It was not until the Enlightenment that a profound change was brought about. Now, all historically transmitted understanding was called into question, and thereby the unity between history and interpretation was broken apart. Of course, talk about mere facticity and the ambiguity of historical data was still a long way off; but people spoke of a new meaning, accessible to enlightened human thought and research, which as it were lay hidden behind the tradition of understanding of earlier, still unenlightened generations, and had now for the first time to be distilled from historical appearances. How that affected the interpretation of the Bible is well known, and does not need to be described here. Obviously, it was only a short step to idealism, with its concept that the Spirit which takes effect in history is self-evident.[6]

The problem became clearer when the rational optimism of the Enlightenment, and also the idealist construction of history, had been broken up. Yet, although the positivist mode of thought was winning more and more adherents, the intellectual attitude of late idealism and the post-idealist period still managed to hold things in a kind of state of suspense for a relatively long time. Not only is that clear from figures like Ernst Troeltsch and Adolf von Harnack,[7] it is also typical of the first edition of the "Handbuch zum Neuen Testament," edited by Hans Lietzmann. For here the application of the historical-critical method (whether already with or still without taking the history of religions into account) could be brought forward as an exegetical program, which as such was unambiguous and, in the lee of liberal theology, offered a clear alternative to any kind of tradition-bound, "conservative" exegesis.

The problem came into sharp focus in the period after the First World War. In this context, we are not primarily concerned with the perspective of dialectical theology, with its new theological approach and the questions it consequently addressed to the method of historical criticism. (Besides Karl Barth's preface to his commentary on the Epistle to the Romans, this perspective emerged from above all in the exchange of letters between Barth and Harnack.)[8]

Our concern is rather with the fact, now admitted openly, quite frankly, and without reserve, that historical data cannot ultimately be illuminated by historical criticism, but in every case remain ambiguous, and their interpretation is therefore a matter of dispute. Of course, that does not exclude the possibility that clear, uncontroversial and perhaps even conclusive statements can be made with respect to particular aspects of historical phenomena. As a rule, however, that applies only to fixing their location with respect to philology, archaeology, and chronology. We already find ourselves in greater difficulty when we set out to describe their conceptual material, their stock of opinions, and their distinctive position in the history of religions or in theology. But the moment we pass beyond the description of facts and aim to give a substantive interpretation of the matters before us, we come up against the controversial nature of all historical occurrences. In the 1920s, the recognition of this fact led to three interesting consequences in the field of exegesis. First, skepticism in principle with respect to historical-critical exegesis, such as we find in Karl Barth, for example. Second, an energetic assault on the question of hermeneutics and a precise integration of it with historical criticism, in Rudolf Bultmann. Finally, a readiness on the part of previously conservative exegetes, and, after a certain interval, of Catholic exegetes as well, to put historical criticism to work in their endeavors. But it followed from this last point, as Ernst Käsemann in particular has remarked more than once, that historical criticism was no longer a method distinctive of a specific kind of exegetical work, but in the field of New Testament research now became a commonly accepted tool of the trade for exegesis.[9] From now on, the way was clear for the use of historical criticism, in the sense of a purely formal, technical method.[10] On the one hand, this seemed justified, indeed inevitable, because the biblical writings are documents of a past era; on the other hand, it provided the opportunity to take up and exploit for exegesis the possibilities and results of the so-called positive sciences, and even in part to contribute to them significantly.

Yet the dilemma that arose in this way may not be overlooked. To dismiss the theological relevance of facts and to concentrate exclusively on the existential interpretation of texts constituted, within exegesis, something like a loss of reality, and in the long run brought a host of theological problems in its wake. Of course, the problems could not be overcome merely by assigning a higher value to facts and to what could be proved historically. This way has been tried by more recent conservative research, which has set out, precisely by means of historical criticism, to establish an ultimately unassailable and obligatory starting point and standard of judgment by going back to the *ipsissima vox Jesu*.[11] But this peculiar continuation of the line of approach of earlier theological liberalism does not do justice to the New Testament, in the first place because there the post-Easter preaching was by no means exclusively measured against Jesus' own message; rather, the adoption of the Jesus tradition took place precisely by way of a process of reception that began with the kerygma. But with respect to the kerygma we do not find a unified picture; instead, there is observable from the very beginning a diversification into different types of early Christian preaching. Thus we do not only encounter controversy over our own interpretation about the meaning of a tradition that we have received; we must also assert that the biblical tradition is strongly differentiated within itself. This problem can be resolved neither by tracing back the different forms of the kerygma to a historically provable, unified phenomenon, nor by starting with a particular concept of the kerygma in the sense of a "canon within the canon" and critically sifting out the other strands of tradition. The state of the problem is considerably more difficult and complex than that.

This briefly sketched process of disintegration, which especially since the time of the Enlightenment had been going on irresistibly, was only temporarily halted by the theology of Bultmann. Undoubtedly, his attempt to bring historical and theological questions into relation with each other was by far the most convincing. But today the integration of history and the kerygma, of the *sensus literalis* and the *sensus propheticus*, of the original tradition of preaching and the history of interpretation is such an open question that we cannot for the moment expect to find a convincing, comprehensive solution, unless we likewise subject our very way of posing the questions, under the influence of which we have come up against these problems, to critical analysis. We cannot clarify and appropriate for ourselves a tradition that grew up under quite different cultural circumstances by increasingly interpreting it on the basis of our own premises, without in the process bringing our own standpoint under critical scrutiny as well. As soon as that happens, we shall recognize that for us today certain questions must necessarily be asked, and we certainly cannot evade them; we shall recognize that it is only when we make allowances for their relativity that we gain proper access to those data whose interpretation we wish to examine.[12] This does not mean that we must set limits to the results of historical-critical research even before they are produced; but we shall have to understand clearly that we may expect no solutions unless we subject the historical-critical method itself to historical criticism. But, having said that, we must begin to face up to the unresolved problems of our method.

II

Identifying the points at which historical criticism has been baffled is probably the most urgent task in exegesis today, because it is only when we have done this that the relation between historical and theological work can be given fresh definition. But since at present we are all still at the task of trying to recognize and demonstrate clearly the state of the problem, we also need to consider in a fundamental way what historical criticism is able to accomplish.

First, there can be no doubt that we are dependent on historical criticism in our exegetical work. That the biblical texts derive from a past era of human history and of human intellectual presuppositions is only one side of this matter. At least as important is the fact that we can recover historical events in a way that is responsible to our own time only if we take into account the possibilities of understanding and knowing in our time. To that extent, it is a task of transmission and of living communication which is posed here. Every process of communication is in this sense bipolar, and necessarily becomes more difficult as the distance is increased between the two poles between which the transmission has to take place. To be sure, this process does not take place only on one plane.

It is at least prepared for by the history of the influence of the earlier pole, even if communication has not actually been kept alive by tradition in a particular form. Thus, with respect to historical criticism, the task of communication arises only in a particularly sophisticated form, the intention of which is to make us aware of hindrances to understanding, and so far as possible to overcome them.

In this very general description of the nature of our task, we have not yet said anything in detail about the efficacy of historical criticism in the sphere of exegesis. In this respect, we must now mention that primary intention which first got the historical-critical method under way, and which we have already encountered: the separation of the text from any tradition of interpretation. Inquiry into the original meaning of every biblical text is indispensable. But the question must be posed and answered with care. For it is not the case that we are simply in possession of the right understanding because of our historical criticism. In one respect, we may be able to approach much more closely the situation and intention of a text; but, in another respect, our access is necessarily limited, and requires constant correction and extension of conclusions that have already been reached. On the other hand, it is also not the case that every tradition of interpretation is conceptually secondary to a supposedly original meaning; for it may allow some quite crucial aspects of the text to make their contribution. Interpretation, in the sense of appropriation with understanding, is an indispensable process, and takes place afresh in every epoch and generation. In many cases, earlier tradition can be nothing but instructive for our own efforts at understanding. Interpretation in the sense of this kind of appropriation really means discovering, even in traditions of interpretation that have become strange to us, by no means only things that must strike us as odd (which of course will be there too) but also those which offer possibilities of access to the text. Every tradition of interpretation contains within itself not only the endeavor to penetrate the text with understanding, but also, in many cases, an opening up of the text which can give us new help. The texts point beyond themselves, and therefore reflection on them should by all means include the dimension of the influence they have exercised. But that does not exclude the need for me at this point to be critical as I make distinctions and sift things, or absolve me from the requirement to observe above all the fundamental distinction between the presupposed text and the tradition of interpretation.

That this distinction between the text and the tradition of interpretation can on the whole be carried through consistently is tied up with another decidedly positive aspect of historical criticism. It puts us into the position where we can to a large extent include in our considerations the presuppositions of the texts and the circumstances in which they came into being. If in the one case we start from the text and march forward down the line of interpretation, and illuminate it, in the other case we walk backward and sideways over the terrain, so to speak, and shed light on it, so that we may be able to describe the historical position of each text with the utmost clarity. We are all sufficiently aware that, despite the abundance of historical material, exegetes are still left with a large number of dark patches. But that should not hinder us from energetically pressing on with historical criticism precisely in this regard, not only so as to complete our picture, to fill in gaps and to dismantle working hypotheses that had temporarily been indispensable, but also so as to explain the texts with ever greater care, precision, and differentiation.

If we walk through the terrain historically in this double direction, then most certainly an illuminating light will fall on the text itself. Historical criticism has contributed, and can contribute further, toward making the distinctive character of the biblical texts known with respect to the history of language, form criticism and redaction criticism, the history of religions, the history of preaching and faith, and, at a preliminary stage, the history of theology. Illuminated by their own situation, the texts turn out to be astonishingly pregnant with meaning. Anyone who completely immerses himself in this study will find that the problems of understanding are to some extent even alleviated by this means, although of course the basic problems of understanding such texts will not yet have been overcome.

But now, can historical-critical exegesis really produce any more results than this? We owe a most interesting and very noteworthy contribution to the question we have just posed to Heinrich Schlier's essay, "What Is the Interpretation of Holy Scripture?"[13] For our purposes, we can leave aside Schlier's opening remarks about the correlation of event and word, and the subsequent comments on the relation between God's self-interpretation and Holy Scripture. In the last part of his essay he turns to the interpretation of Scripture and speaks of three distinct guidelines which are imposed on interpretation by the distinctive character of the text. In summary, the first guideline corresponds to what we have just been discussing: the interpretation of Scripture as a historical document calls for historical method, and also shares with it the uncertainty of historical access to reality. "But that does not absolve interpretation from its task of methodically setting forth Holy Scripture's historical text as such (for we find that it turns out to be a historical text) in its historical peculiarity, and allowing it (that is, Holy Scripture) in just this way to cast its first glance toward us or even to address the first word to us." This brings Schlier to his second guideline, and, for the question we have before us at the moment, this step is the most important. If the historical peculiarity of the text is recognized, then it turns out to be the document of a claim — "the claim which was issued in God's self-interpretation in Jesus Christ and is now issued in Scripture." To that extent, we are required to follow the intention of Scripture, "which presents itself to us in the form and content of its text." "The goal of interpretation must be to appropriate God's claim, which is made with and in Scripture; for this claim, and nothing else, is the truth of Scripture." If we do not perceive and expose the truth of this history presented in Scripture, such as the truth of the historical fact of Jesus' crucifixion, then all that we encounter is an "abstraction of history." "But as soon as that happens, the fact, as something historical, also disappears. For a historical fact is such, in itself and in its historical effect, only when it is interpreted." Then come the crucial sentences: "Interpretation today must of course bring this state of affairs to light by means of historical method, for example, especially through form criticism. But if it wishes to give contemporary expression to the truth of this death, in accordance with the intention of the gospels, then it must allow this event to encounter our understanding in its *truth*: that is, it must interpret this event as one which, through the interpretation, has been disclosed in its truth." To be sure, that presupposes "an understanding which is affected by the subject matter, and which affects it, an understanding which opens itself up in unselfconscious, living, obedient hearing." The third guideline, which we need only touch on in passing, refers to the ecclesiastical tradition of interpretation; for, according to Schlier, the church is "the sphere in which the claim of the event of revelation has always been heard already, in order always to be heard anew." Therefore, every individual act of interpretation is partly constituted by interpretations which have preceded it and by interpretations which will follow. What we must be particularly concerned with is the portrayal here of a remarkably smooth transition from the historical-critical description of the particular character of biblical texts to that claim which, in Schlier's view, can be recognized precisely in the context of that careful description, and which not only requires one to accept it personally as truth, but also must become the goal of any interpretation. In Schlier's scheme, dogmatics and preaching of course come into their own as well, tied up as they are with the understanding conveyed by the ecclesiastical tradition of interpretation. That necessarily brings us into the sphere of contemporary, practical problems; but still the constitutive factor remains the "approach to that word," namely, the word of Scripture. For exegesis is concerned with the fundamental "claim issued by God's truth in Scripture for every age." We may observe in passing (and I find this most revealing) how Schlier has here combined his inheritance from the Reformation with his Catholic sense of tradition: but, that apart, the essential question remains whether we are really able to combine historical and theological interpretation in this way.

As soon as we look into the execution of this task, we shall see that the answer must certainly be no — because this suggestion has been too quick to turn the lights down, or even switch them off altogether, on problems both of history on the one hand and of theology and hermeneutics on the other. Nevertheless, we must consider whether Schlier, by so strongly emphasizing the convergence of historical and theological concerns of past and present interpretations, does not have something very important in view. Peter

Stuhlmacher has something similar in mind when he argues that the three principles named by Troeltsch, criticism, correlation, and analogy, must be supplemented by a fourth, that of "appropriation" or "consent."[14] But for the time being that is at best a programmatic suggestion, as Stuhlmacher himself clearly recognizes, not a solution of the problem. A proposal like Schlier's, which at first sight looks so well-balanced, may tend to diminish the urgency of our inquiry, and that would not be helpful for our situation. For the historical-critical analysis of the New Testament by no means leads us so clearly in the direction indicated by him, but presents a most confusing picture. There can be no question that at this point Bultmann saw the issue more acutely, when in his hermeneutic concept he decided not to keep following along the line prescribed by historical criticism, but looked for a point of departure that was ultimately independent of it. What the historical-critical method can do is to demonstrate how the form which the proclamation takes in each age is historically conditioned; in addition, it is able to define the central contents and the modes of expression of the early Christian message, but on its own is not in a position really to do justice to the intention of the texts. Of course, without wishing to tie up the decision of faith itself into a system, a method of biblical exegesis ought to be able to take the substantive claim of the texts into account and expose it to view, since only in that way will it be fully appropriate to its subject matter. But historical-critical exegesis in the form in which we know it is not in a position to do that. One might want to follow the method attempted by Schlier, by continuing straight on from historical criticism and, building on that foundation, bringing in the question of truth. But then one would first have to consider whether that is actually possible by the usual approaches, or whether one will not have to make a prior, fundamental examination of the latent premises, principles, and countless imponderables in our historical-critical method.

III

Now we must at last turn our attention to the points of perplexity in historical criticism. It would be a good idea to begin by explicitly recalling the fact that historical criticism is itself a historical phenomenon, and that before its time there had been a long history of interpretation, which was both intensive and fruitful. In his above-mentioned essay on "the hermeneutic scope of historical-critical exegesis," Karl Lehmann observes that one often gets the impression these days that, although the historical-critical method is recognized as being a modern achievement, it is thought of in a peculiarly unhistorical way.[15] Our point at the moment is not just that modern historical criticism appeared in quite particular circumstances in intellectual history and kept on developing. The main point is that it is by no means a fixed entity before which one must simply bow down uncritically; instead, we must check whether it still does justice, in the form which it has taken in history, to the contemporary intellectual situation, and especially to the task of exegesis.

That brings us at once to an important problem, that of the much-invoked "lack of presuppositions" in historical criticism as a modern scholarly method. It may be granted completely that the historical-critical method within the biblical exegesis of the past two hundred years has shown an astonishing flexibility, and to a large extent has been capable of adaptation both to the special situation with regard to sources and to the specific character of the biblical writings; hence it has become a really useful and versatile tool. But, despite this adaptability, the fact remains that the supposed lack of presuppositions was a positivist axiom which has long since proved to be untenable. Instead, the flexibility allowed people repeatedly to delude themselves about their premises, which were taken over without reflection and accordingly took effect only in a latent way. But the premises of historical criticism have long-lasting consequences, as can easily be demonstrated at three points, which really deserve thorough attention with respect to methodology and the history of theology but have so far not received it.

First, there is the concept of autonomous human reason, which has been unreflectively adopted as a criterion. This concept of reason became possible only in a quite special set of circumstances in modern intellectual history. When it, with all its consequences, is applied to past human history and thought, tensions necessarily arise, and these should be acknowledged and laid open for discussion to a far greater extent than has so far happened. This is particularly needed because it is a quite open question whether this concept of reason, which has largely dominated the period from the eighteenth to the twentieth century, can be of much further use in coping with the tasks confronting humanity. To say the least, people concerned with exegesis should be taking a much more intensive interest in the biblical concept of reason and its relation to our modern thought, and this should form an essential part of our consideration of methodological problems.

The same is true of the modern understanding of reality. This is without doubt extremely complex, and we should beware of hasty attempts to simplify it. Bultmann has always been accused of starting with a concept of reality that was already out of date.[16] However that may be, he was at least setting out to bring a typically modern way of thinking (and indeed a modern way of thinking that had already become popular) into relation with the historical analysis of the texts on the one hand, and with his hermeneutic initiative on the other. But much more really needs to be done here, if there is to be any fruitful encounter between different perceptions of reality, and if the modern understanding of reality, which is constantly shifting, is to receive from the biblical message new impulses which it will be able to integrate along with others.

Finally, we should also raise questions about important elements in the contemporary understanding of history and the future; here too we should bring this understanding into relation with the biblical view of history and the future, and from that perspective reexamine the one-sided way in which the historical-critical method looks only backwards in its concept of history. The fact that for many people today historical study has become uninteresting and that the results of historical research are ignored, indeed that history itself and its handing-on are pushed aside, may be due not least to the fact that our traditional modern approach to history is dominated by presuppositions which are no longer adequate for the tasks of the present and the future.[17]

But I do not wish to keep on developing these reflections on the general premises of historical criticism, which have become so problematic. Instead, I would like to take up two matters that are obviously connected with points of perplexity in our method. With respect to our situation, the problems involved here are particularly significant ones; but, remarkably, they are scarcely ever discussed.

The historical-critical analysis of texts has a decidedly alienating effect. No one has emphasized this more impressively than Albert Schweitzer in his concluding reflection on the quest of the historical Jesus: "A curious thing has happened to research into the life of Jesus. It set out in quest of the historical Jesus, believing that when it had found him it could bring him straight into our time as Teacher and Saviour. It loosed the bands by which for centuries he had been chained to the rocks of ecclesiastical doctrine, and rejoiced when life and movement came into the figure once more, and it could see the historical man Jesus coming to meet it. But he did not stay: he passed by our time and returned to his own."[18] Without doubt, this alienation of texts has a positive aspect. For it has repeatedly given rise to new reflections; it has removed the tradition from the sphere of things which are all too well known and familiar, and which have come to be taken for granted; and it has brought to light the independence of the biblical text from any attempt to understand and appropriate it. Yet Albert Schweitzer also emphasized, and not without reason, the negative side of this act of alienation: the conscious erection of a barrier of historical distance. Naturally one can point out, indeed one must point out, that the biblical texts make their strangeness obvious to the reader, especially the reader who stands at a distance from the church's tradition: and this primarily happens not in central things, but first of all in things on the periphery. Nevertheless, it must be realized that historical criticism stabilizes this strangeness and distance. But, in so doing, it runs directly contrary to the intention of the text: and in biblical exegesis that should not be forgotten. For the interest of the texts is not in a historical consciousness. Even in cases where distance has already been felt and reflected on, they are each respectively addressed to the present time. They are not only open to the present; their decisive aspect is their reference to the present. This explains the mode of portraying the past which is so distinctive of the Old and New Testaments. The past is reported for the sake of the present, and in every case it is brought into relation with the present. There are important theological reasons for this; in the New Testament, these are the confession of the One who is risen and exalted, and awareness of the activity of the Spirit. This has left its mark even on the structure of the texts. At this point that distancing, objectifying procedure of historical criticism does not do justice to the tendency and the explicit aims of the texts that have come down to us. Hence there arise hermeneutic problems, which are really caused in the first place by a way of handling the texts that is ultimately inadequate. Here we should be checking whether this method that sets up a barrier of distance is not determined by premises that are out of place. Obviously, saying that does not get rid of the problem that we are dealing with texts almost two thousand years old. But it does make a difference whether piers for the bridge of understanding are being demolished or whether they are being made visible and being reinforced. The image I have just used should make it clear that I am very far from expecting that the historical approach on its own will bring me to a real understanding. The understanding of an alleged state of affairs can certainly not dispense with historical analysis, because this is the only way in which it is possible to grasp precisely what texts are saying. All the same, interpretation may not disregard the all-important claim which includes in its scope the contemporary situation in each case. Historical criticism performs its specific function only within the framework of a comprehensive process of understanding. It is not confined to preparing the way for the correct understanding, but also makes an essential contribution to the correct definition of the subject matter.

In addition to emphasizing distance, historical criticism carries with it a tendency toward isolation. By that, I do not mean complete separation from a set of circumstances, but that the specific incident or the individual text being dealt with is narrowed down to its determinative elements and described in these terms. Correspondingly, when a comprehensive presentation is made, the recognizable and possible causal connections between individual events or texts are pointed out. But transcendent points of reference are systematically excluded by this approach. And that is why a history of Israel or a history of early Christianity forms such a striking contrast to any kind of biblical historiography. I certainly do not wish to deny that there inevitably will be quite diverse points of view and modes of presentation. But can historical research and criticism move so far away from the perspective which is clearly essential to the biblical understanding of history (despite considerable variation and divergence within that understanding), so as to replace it with a view which is purely causal and correlative? I am skeptical about any attempt to use some kind of framework of universal history for interpretation. Even where certain universalist tendencies are discernible in the biblical writings, there was, in my opinion, no attempt anywhere in the Bible to write a really "universal history." Much more distinctive of the biblical view of history is the fact that quite particular, individual events are brought forward as reference points which give direction to broad periods of time, and that this is the basis for the arrangement of the material and the answers given to historical questions and historical thinking. This "perspectivist" outlook, as I should like to call it, seems to me to take us further than any proposal based on evolutionary history, because the perspectivist outlook remains much more open for the understanding and contemplation of historical reality.[19] It is very far from being a settled question, whether the ostensible renunciation of a transcendent outlook and the consequent predominance of a causal and correlative explanation of historical phenomena is really more appropriate to the problem and to the understanding of history. Examples in the Old Testament of reference points which had the function of giving direction were the stories of Abraham and of the Exodus. In the New Testament it is primarily the public activity, death, and resurrection of Jesus. The problem of isolation that I have indicated carries with it a further consequence: because at the outset every phenomenon is explained simply with reference to itself, no attention is paid to the fact that precisely those historical phenomena which have taken on the function of giving direction obviously do not admit of just any interpretation, but require either the acceptance or the rejection of a quite particular explanation. When I speak of a quite particular explanation, that does not mean a unified explanation in every case, but an understanding which does however admit of only a certain range of explanation and a particular scope for variability. In this connection, the task of examining and arranging the material by means of new categories is, I suggest, one as urgent as it would be rewarding.

In addition, as I have already indicated, historical criticism, as applied to the analysis of biblical texts, lacks not only the dimension of the present but also that of the future. It can indeed describe how the future was seen by an earlier time, a time which for us lies in the past, but again it can offer no possibility of comprehending, in anything like an appropriate way, the energy and continuing impulses of these earlier expectations of the future.

It is precisely the biblical tradition which should make it possible for us to recognize the decidedly defective view of history that has set its mark on historical criticism, and to a large extent continues to govern it. Until we can get rid of these inadequate, indeed obstructive premises, we shall not be able to find our way out of the impasses of contemporary exegesis. Until we do that, there is no use in trying to get around the dilemma by some such path as that sought by Schlier; the divergence has become too great for reestablishing the link between the historical and the theological task of exegesis in that way. Only when by historical analysis and by hermeneutic effort we have found a new and solid basis will the work of exegesis be able to fulfill its service to the church in the right way. For the time being, we can admittedly offer no solutions — but first of all we must face up to the problems that have brought us into perplexity.

NOTES

1. Characteristic of this point of view is the book by Heinrich Zimmermann, *Neutestamentliche Methodenlehre. Darstellung der historisch-kritischen Methode*, 2nd ed. (Stuttgart: Verlag Katholisches Bibelwerk, 1968), esp. the introduction, pp. 17ff., and the postscript, pp. 258ff.

2. This is emphasized by James M. Robinson and Helmut Koester, *Trajectories through Early Christianity* (Philadelphia: Fortress Press, 1971).

They see the crisis in contemporary exegetical research above all in the categories and historical schemata which till then had been employed. In their opinion, discussion of "trajectories" must replace questions about "background" and the different "positions"; these "trajectories" would then dispense, e.g., with the need for a distinction between Jewish, Christian, and Gnostic apocalyptic, or between canonical and noncanonical tradition (see esp. pp. 8 ff.). But this idea is not so new, if one thinks of the methodological approach of Gustav Krüger, *Geschichte der altchristlichen Literatur in den ersten drei Jahrhunderten*, 2nd ed. (Freiburg and Leipzig: J. C. B. Mohr, 1898) and of William Wrede, *Über Aufgabe und Methode der sogenannten neutestamentlichen Theologie* (Göttingen: Vandenhoeck & Ruprecht, 1897); ET in Robert Morgan, *The Nature of New Testament Theology*, SBT, Second Series 25 (Naperville, Ill.: Alec R. Allenson, 1973), pp. 68–116. With respect to the position of pre-Christian Judaism in relation to its environment, it is surprising that Robinson and Koester make no mention of Martin Hengel's outstanding 1969 book, later published in ET as *Judaism and Hellenism* (Philadelphia: Fortress Press, 1974). Moreover, just as in church history, one will not be able to dispense with so-called cross sections, in addition to trajectories, if one wishes to describe the complicated state of affairs when dealing with the earliest stages of Christianity. Then, too, the concept of development, which dominates very strongly, surely needs to be reconsidered.

3. See Peter Stuhlmacher, "Neues Testament und Hermeneutik — Versuch einer Bestandaufnahme," *ZThK* 68 (1971): 121–61; "Zur Methoden- und Sachproblematik einer interkonfessionellen Auslegung des Neuen Testaments," in *Evangelisch-Katholischer Kommentar zum Neuen Testament*, Vorarbeiten 4 (Neukirchen-Vluyn: Neukirchener Verlag, 1972), 1–55; "Thesen zur Methodologie gegenwärtiger Exegese," *ZNW* 63 (1972): 18–26; *Historical Criticism and Theological Interpretation of Scripture: Toward a Hermeneutics of Consent* (Philadelphia: Fortress Press, 1977); "Adolf Schlatter's Interpretation of Scripture," *NTS* 24 (1977–78): 433–46.

4. We may simply refer to Rudolf Bultmann, *Jesus Christ and Mythology* (New York: Harper & Brothers, 1958), esp. pp. 83ff.; Gerhard Ebeling, "The Significance of the Critical Historical Method for Church and Theology in Protestantism," in *Word and Faith* (Philadelphia: Fortress Press, 1963), pp. 17–61, esp. pp. 49ff.

5. There is some material, with bibliographical references, in Stuhlmacher, "Neues Testament und Hermeneutik," pp. 123ff., and — in more detail — in *Historical Criticism*, pp. 22–60.

6. On the importance of Ferdinand Christian Baur for the development and use of the historical-critical method, see the instructive essay by Heinz Liebing, "Historisch-kritische Theologie. Zum 100. Todestag Ferdinand Christian Baurs am 2. Dezember 1960," *ZThK* 57 (1960): 302–17.

7. Typical are above all Ernst Troeltsch, "Über historische und

dogmatische Methode in der Theologie" (1898; now in *Theologie als Wissenschaft*, ed. Gerhard Sauter, ThB 43 [Munich: Chr. Kaiser Verlag, 1971], pp. 105–27), and Adolf von Harnack, *What is Christianity?* (New York: Harper & Brothers, 1957).

8. Both are in the collection *Anfänge der dialektischen Theologie*, vol. 1, 2nd. ed., ed. Jürgen Moltmann, ThB 17 (Munich: Chr. Kaiser Verlag, 1966).

9. See Ernst Käsemann, "The Problem of the Historical Jesus," in *Essays on New Testament Themes*, SBT 41 (Naperville, Ill.: Alec R. Allenson, 1964), pp. 15–47, esp. p. 17; *The Testimony of Jesus* (Philadelphia: Fortress Press, 1968), pp. 8, 28.

10. See Karl Lehmann, "Der hermeneutische Horizont der historisch-kritischen Exegese," in *Einführung in die Methoden der biblischen Exegese*, ed. Josef Schreiner (Würzburg: Echter Verlag, 1971), pp. 40–80, esp. pp. 63f.

11. Typical of this are the works of Joachim Jeremias, *The Problem of the Historical Jesus*, Facet Books, Biblical Series 13 (Philadelphia: Fortress Press, 1964) and *New Testament Theology: The Proclamation of Jesus* (New York: Charles Scribner's Sons, 1971). Criticism of his theological approach does not cancel out the great importance of his contribution to research on the problem of the historical Jesus.

12. That is rightly emphasized in the important essay by Karl Lehmann. "Historical objectivism, or positivism, went astray in that, although it recognized that the object is affected by historical influences, it did not recognize that the understanding subject has the same mode of existence" ("Der hermeneutische Horizont der historisch-kritischen Exegese," p. 61).

13. Heinrich Schlier, "Was heisst Auslegung der Heiligen Schrift?" (1964), in *Besinnung auf das Neue Testament. Exegetische Aufsätze und Vorträge*, vol. 2 (Freiburg im Breisgau: Herder Verlag, 1964), pp. 35–62. The subsequent quotations come from pp. 52f., 55, 58, 61f.

14. Stuhlmacher, "Neues Testament und Hermeneutik," pp. 148f. See "Kritische Marginalien zum gegenwärtigen Stand der Frage nach Jesus," in *Fides et Communicatio. Festschrift für Martin Doerne*, ed. Dietrich Rössler, Gottfried Voigt, and Friedrich Wente (Göttingen: Vandenhoeck & Ruprecht, 1970), pp. 36ff.; *Historical Criticism*, pp. 83ff.

15. Lehmann, "Der hermeneutische Horizont der historisch-kritischen Exegese," p. 59; but see also his remarks on pp. 58ff., 75ff.

16. This applies especially to the presentation of the mythical worldview in the first part of Rudolf Bultmann's essay, "New Testament and Mythology" (1941), in *Kerygma and Myth*, ed. Hans Werner Bartsch (London: SPCK, 1953), pp. 1–44.

17. In this respect, the first signs of a change are now evident; let us simply refer to the discussion inaugurated by the publication of Jürgen Moltmann, *Theology of Hope* (New York: Harper & Row, 1967) and

NOTES **33**

Gerhard Sauter, *Zukunft und Verheissung* (Zurich and Stuttgart: Zwingli Verlag, 1965). In the background there are impulses that originated in exegesis.

18. Albert Schweitzer, *The Quest of the Historical Jesus* (New York: Macmillan, 1968), p. 399. [Translator's note: W. Montgomery's rendering of this well-known passage in the English edition of Schweitzer's book has here been amended. In particular, Montgomery's unwarranted use of present-tense verbs in the last sentence would have been rather seriously misleading, in the context of Professor Hahn's argument.]

19. The use of the Old Testament in the New should be examined along the lines of such a perspectivist outlook; I suspect that that would lead us out of many barren bypaths.

METHODOLOGICAL REFLECTIONS ON THE HISTORICAL INVESTIGATION OF JESUS

THERE ARE QUESTIONS in theology which never leave us alone; questions which keep pressing themselves upon us and which must constantly be posed afresh. Their urgency does not depend primarily on whether such questions have previously received satisfactory or inadequate answers; of course, results already attained can be pushed further, and the problems can always be made to yield new insights. More importantly, there are questions which keep theological thought as such on the move; they are therefore questions on which we can never give up. On the contrary, we must beware of letting ourselves be satisfied with the answers already given. Our task is rather to keep subjecting the proposed solutions to regular reexamination, without however letting ourselves be bogged down at the point of mere questioning. Theology fulfills its task when it remains in the constant interplay of question and answer, when it does not merely see itself as released from answers given in the past, but out of questions addressed to the present time comes to its own new answers. Only so does theology fulfill its duty to the church, because for the church contemporary responsibility is always of decisive importance.

The problems which keep theological thought on the move are not posed in the same way in all periods. But there is no doubt that the question of the history and person of Jesus is today among those basic questions which are not to be avoided and which do not let us go. It is by no means only the specialists in exegesis who are involved here; the question has become a pivotal point for interdisciplinary discussion in theology. It also belongs just as much to the church's general education and understanding of the faith, and moreover marks the neuralgic point of any genuine conversation between Christians and non-Christians.[1]

If therefore this question has a significance that extends far beyond our own discipline, we specialists in New Testament exegesis are faced with the task of working over this field of study, with regard to both method and substance, in such a way that the tracks are properly set for theological discussion in general, so that (to continue the metaphor) we may not keep having railroad accidents or having vehicles shunted onto the sidetracks.

In what follows, I wish to strive after basic clarifications of method. It will be seen that questions of method can be isolated only to a certain degree. They cannot be dealt with in the sense of general formal principles and preliminary questions of neutral import. The discussion of problems of method is always closely bound up with the analysis and interpretation of the texts, because every method must be developed, or at least refined, with reference to the subject matter to be investigated. An adequate methodological procedure cannot be laid down in advance, but needs constant testing and checking on the field of inquiry. But that is not enough. In the case of texts which are relevant for faith, attention must also be paid in each case to the theological significance of the methodological procedure and of the results obtained through it. This has to do not only with a secondary "application" of the method and of the results it produces for the inquiry, but also with the understanding of the method itself, which, despite a range of points of view from which the text may be examined, can never ignore the specific character of its subject matter. Nevertheless, three closely related steps may be distinguished, and are discussed in the three parts that follow. My aim is to deal first with the difficulties involved in getting back to the pre-Easter Jesus, then to speak of the positive possibilities of getting back to the history of Jesus, and finally to explain why a historical investigation of Jesus is justified from the point of view of relevance.

DIFFICULTIES OF THE INVESTIGATION

The difficulties of reaching back historically to the pre-Easter Jesus are quite familiar to anyone who is intensively occupied with the problem. Yet it is surprising that no comprehensive account exists of the vexing questions facing this branch of exegesis.[2] Moreover, it must be said that extreme positions are frequently taken up, which are by no means appropriate to the complicated facts of the case. Thus people sometimes adopt too hastily the hypothesis that it is virtually impossible to break through historically to the pre-Easter Jesus;[3] or else they underestimate the difficulties involved, and suppose they are dealing with biographical material, so as to sketch, with the aid of the gospel tradition as we have it, the most detailed possible picture of the history of Jesus.[4] If there is any discussion of the difficulties at all, it takes place almost exclusively in relation to the history of research. Yet to give our attention to research on the historical Jesus in the last two hundred years is clearly not enough. Such discussion can indeed open up for us important insights into the various premises with which scholars have worked, and into their different ways of handling the sources; but it does not sufficiently bring to light the fundamental problems which are unavoidably posed in our work at all times.[5]

We therefore cannot avoid grappling with the abiding perplexities; we need at the same time a thoroughgoing, detailed theory of criteria, which will make the establishment of the material in the pre-Easter tradition meaningful and verifiable.[6] Only in this way can we escape from the dilemma of either simply denying the possibility of getting back to the pre-Easter Jesus, or else asserting it at the cost of short-circuiting the problems. What I am now proposing in this discussion is meant simply to provide a starting point and to make clear the urgency of the task.

In exegetical work the difficulties arise especially at three points: first, in the selection of the tradition about Jesus, then in the formal shaping and reshaping of the tradition within the New Testament, and finally in its reinterpretation.

Selection of the Tradition About Jesus

With respect to selection we must take quite different strata into account:

1. When we compare Matthew and Luke with Mark, we observe that the two later evangelists have not taken over the whole material. They have indeed followed their source to a large extent,

yet they have made abbreviations and omissions.[7] The same problem occurs of course in their treatment of the Sayings source: in
several passages we have reason to ask whether material which remains preserved in only one gospel should not be assigned to the
Q tradition; and therefore it is extremely difficult, in a number of
passages, to distinguish between material from Q and from the
evangelist's own special source.[8] What holds true for Matthew and
Luke must also be presumed for Mark: in any written compilation
of the traditional material there takes place not simply a collecting
of the existing data but also a selection from what is available.
Though what is omitted may be slight in comparison with what
is taken over, it must not be left out of consideration or regarded
as insignificant.[9]

2. It is not only in the case of the gospels (that is, the process
in which the tradition was reduced to written form) that material
was collected and at the same time cautiously subjected to selection: the same process had already occurred in the oral tradition
at every stage in which an effort was made to collect and set in
order sayings of Jesus or narratives about him. But this selective
procedure was carried out not just once, as in the composition of
a gospel: it could take place throughout the whole period of oral
transmission. If there was less occasion for this in a simple stringing-
together of the material than in a planned compilation of
thematically related matter, we must in any case reckon with the
possibility that material could be not only incorporated but also,
for whatever reasons, discarded.[10]

3. A further significant occasion for selection was provided by
the transition from the Aramaic to the Greek linguistic sphere. At
this point there could well have taken place a not insignificant process of rejection. It should not be forgotten that our knowledge of
the Aramaic-speaking churches of Palestine in the post-Easter period
depends entirely on the preservation of their traditions by the Greek-
speaking churches. The traditions so preserved are, as we all know,
extremely scanty. The same does not have to hold true, a priori,
of the tradition about Jesus. Yet we must presume that original traditions about Jesus which were current in the churches of the
Aramaic-speaking area were not taken over in their full extent; this

would have happened, moreover, no matter how we define the relationship between the Aramaic- and the Greek-speaking churches. For, at some point or other, the translation had to be effected, irrespective of the shaping and arrangement of the Jesus material in the various branches of tradition, since the original stock deriving from Jesus was in any case in Aramaic. The reduction may have been due to purely linguistic reasons, since particular sayings were hard to translate and outside the environment of Aramaic speech were scarcely comprehensible; but it may also have been due to the contents.[11] It is indisputable that Aramaisms and some sayings hard to understand were dragged along in the later tradition, but this argument should not induce us to deny too hastily that selection was bound up with the process of translation.[12]

4. Finally, we must take into account a not inconsiderable loss of material in the transition from the time before Easter to the church's tradition after Easter. At this point the much-discussed question of the significance of the "Easter rift"[13] does not need to be played up; by the change in the situation from before to after Easter it was inevitable that sayings of Jesus and reports about his deeds should have been lost. That remains true, even if we may assume that there was considerable interest in the pre-Easter tradition and even if we presuppose that the process of transmission began in Jesus' lifetime.[14] We must at the least presume that the effort to reach back to what happened before Easter was not made in all church groups (former disciples and new converts) with the same intensity and with the same purpose: and this must have led to a certain selection.

This fourfold process by which the original stock of tradition was reduced must not be disregarded. It cannot be objected that this process of selection can really be demonstrated only in the redaction of our existing gospels; in groups of sayings, too, it is still discernible. Moreover, in a methodology, matters which can only be deduced by analogy must be taken into consideration, because otherwise the total conception which arises can easily be false. That is, we must depict for ourselves the possible circumstances of transmission clearly enough so that we can correctly integrate the actual data. At all events, in doing this we must take seriously the *fragmentary character* of the surviving tradition, especially of the tradition from the time before Easter.[15] For this reason we must beware of hastening to the view that the available material is a unified fabric. Only with the redactional composition of the gospels did it receive a relative unity. Apart from that, particular attention must be paid to the variety of forms and to the different strata of historical depth. With regard to the perspective of depth, the person of Jesus is not only the unique point of departure but also the permanent focus. So in addition to the dimension of breadth, which has been gradually established, precisely that stratification of depth is especially important: but it presumes a precise differentiation in the history of transmission, which must take the loss of traditions just as much into account as the development of traditions.

The reflections we have made so far do not by any means imply a simply negative outcome. The positive function of these methodological considerations must not be underrated. For this function is linked with the recognition that the "narrrowing down" observable since Easter is not confined to the development of the Christological proclamation, which did indeed, as is well known, set in motion a new, very fruitful process of transmission.[16] Rather, it is to be seen in the deliberate concentration on certain main lines of Jesus' preaching and also on actions and disputes which continued to be of relevance for the church.[17] Yet precisely those elements of the genuine Jesus material which do not readily fit in with this interest, and now create the impression of standing somewhat on the margin, can open up for us insights into some potentially important sectors of the activity of Jesus. But here we cannot reach a conclusive judgment without effort, for the necessary context is simply no longer available to us, or we have it only in fragmentary form.[18]

Shaping and Reshaping of the Jesus Tradition

It is not only of interest to know *what* survived: we must also examine *how* the Jesus tradition was preserved. That brings us up against the problems of shaping literary form in transmission [*Formgebung*].

The intrinsic tendency in the transmission was unquestionably to collect and preserve: nevertheless, as we have already seen, there also arose the need for a certain degree of selection and rejection. Where there exists an interest in preservation, the process of collection takes place automatically, so to speak. If the transmission of individual sayings and deeds of Jesus is carried out with the intention that they should be conserved and handed on to others, this very act of transmitting them implies that they are destined for collection. The process of collection begins consciously wherever transmitted materials are linked together and combined into units.[19]

As in all oral tradition, the material's preservation is assisted by the form given to it. Formal characteristics provide the preconditions for transmission without the risk of arbitrary tampering. At the same time the form expresses the intention governing the transmission, and thus reveals the concrete *Sitz im Leben* ("life situation").[20]

But shaping into a form is by no means merely a subsequent process of fusion. Every piece of material requires an adequate external form, which has an important influence right from the beginning. So from the outset sayings of Jesus must have had a particular form, which could be maintained and handed on essentially unchanged. Consequently, despite fairly strong dependence on the medium of the narrator, stories about Jesus retained a basic shaping, which is most important for understanding them. However, the process of shaping does not simply cease when the material to be preserved has once reached its relatively fixed outlines. The alterations which take place subsequently may seem to be minimal, but they should by no means be overlooked. For preservation occurs precisely in such a way that the material in question is adapted, and handed on in this adapted form. As long as oral tradition continues, shaping of form is a living process, in which the life situations responsible for the transmission share in molding the material.[21] That is most clearly obvious to us through the deliberate incorporation of the Jesus tradition into the early church's Christological preaching;[22] but it is still plainly recognizable at other levels as well.

In our historical search for authentic traditions about Jesus, we must determine how far this process of shaping, in both its original and subsequent stages, can be traced by distinct signs. For it is only when stages in the transmission after Jesus can be definitely established that we can gain access to Jesus himself. Once again we can observe the process at four different stages:

1. A glance into the gospels reveals that the way in which individual pieces of tradition occur in the respective gospels is subject to alterations with respect to both form and language, and thus shares to a not inconsiderable degree the imprint of the Marcan, Matthean, Lucan, or Johannine "style."[23] If we leave aside the question of how far this is a matter of the particular character of each evangelist, even the material taken over from tradition was subject to the influence of a distinct manner of presentation, as can be most clearly observed in the Johannine tradition. We must therefore accept the fact that each piece of tradition was exposed to a considerable process of formal modification.

2. Moreover, as elements were accumulated over the course of several decades, the attempt was made to assimilate them formally to one another, as complexes of traditions were formed. That applies not only to the "schematization" of the miracle stories, where the standard forms are the expression of an easily discernible intention in the transmission. In the Sayings tradition, too, we can detect cases where sayings are formed by analogy, and this is not necessarily an indication of originality. It may instead be a sign of later assimilation and revision.[24] In any case, with respect to the formal shaping, we must pay attention to the complete fabric, which facilitated preservation; we must also pay particular attention to the alterations, which increasingly standardized the material within a strand of tradition, although this process was slow and incomplete.

3. In this connection we must recall once more the translation from Aramaic to Greek and the difficulties arising therefrom. Without doubt there was in Hellenistic Judaism a long tradition of the rendering of Hebrew-Aramaic speech forms into Greek idiom. But it is precisely from the extant documents of Hellenistic Judaism that we can clearly infer how laborious the reproduction was in many cases, and how easily the danger of an unintended Helleniza-

tion arose.[25] We possess no texts at all through which we can check the Jesus tradition against some written Aramaic source. We are only able to use certain indicators to check the Aramaic character of the sayings of Jesus as we have them. But here we have to pay regard to the unsettled question of which dialect Jesus spoke, and which sources may be used to describe it in detail.[26] We know that the number of sayings which can be retranslated with some degree of certainty is very small, although traces of Aramaic expression have been preserved relatively often.

4. Finally, we must take into account the fact that in the transition from the time before to the time after Easter, a new mode of transmission necessarily emerged. If we presume not only that Jesus himself had a decisive part in the formal shaping of his teachings, but also that first steps toward the establishment of a tradition may have been taken within the circle of his disciples, then it follows that the outlines were formed in Jesus' lifetime and under the immediate influence of his own activity.[27] However, after his death and resurrection the material was collected and handed on within an altered frame of reference and orientation. For on the one hand it was now a tradition that was consciously traced back to a figure of the past, but on the other hand this tradition was borne along by knowledge of the presence and living power of the risen Lord, whether this was stated explicitly or not.[28] This relationship could not remain without affecting the formation of the material, and necessarily led to not inconsiderable reshaping. Moreover, the actual Christological proclamation increasingly affected the formal shaping.

We are thus confronted by the fact, not always sufficiently appreciated, that we no longer possess in its original form that tradition about Jesus which originated in the time after Easter and was handed on in connection with the establishment of the church and with its mission. On the contrary, despite the partially original shaping, the post-Easter situation caused considerable alterations.

Despite these observations, which claim our attention with respect to method, it must also be said, on the other side, that in many cases the distinctive character of Jesus' sayings has manifestly been preserved, even in their linguistic and formal shape. Moreover, the character of numerous sayings was already predetermined by Jesus, and in the form they were given after Easter foreign models were not simply picked up and imposed roughly on them. Despite all the recasting, they were deliberately assimilated to the genuine Jesus tradition. Finally, despite the process of translation, it is clearly discernible that an earlier transmission in Aramaic stands in the background and still permits us to draw inferences.[29] Hence we can establish that on the one hand quite ancient elements were taken up, and on the other hand, in isolated cases, the distance from the original Jesus tradition with respect to form is surprisingly great.[30] But that only becomes clear when the whole process of the formation of tradition is kept in view: that is, when we can see both the way in which the transmitted material was modified and also how adherence to the basic Jesus tradition was both aimed at and actually achieved.

As a point of method, both these aspects must be observed; they must be taken seriously, despite the tension which undeniably exists between them, and be brought critically into account in the analysis of each individual element of the tradition. Admittedly, it can then be seen how hard it will be in many passages to make a conclusive statement about the original form of a saying of the Lord, even if the component parts of its contents are to a large extent clear. The more cautiously we pass judgment here, and the more painstakingly we distinguish between conclusions which are relatively certain, less certain, and only conjectural, the more helpful it will be for the whole task; and in the long run we shall by these means achieve not less, but more for the recovery of the genuine Jesus material.

Reinterpretation of the Jesus Tradition

Because of the close connection between factors of form and substance, the question of shaping and reshaping in the outlines of the transmitted material has already brought us to the alterations and new turns in interpretation which were taking place at the same time. Naturally, such interpretations were looked on not as a surrender to foreign influence, but as adding depth: hence they should be regarded by us, too, in this light. Nevertheless, there is an obstacle which cannot easily be waved aside on the way to our goal of reaching back to the pre-Easter Jesus. We must now apply ourselves directly to what is without doubt the most difficult and important problem of reinterpretation: again let us do so in several steps, although this time the transition from the Aramaic to the Greek sphere of tradition can be disregarded.

1. Once more we need only compare the gospel texts with one another to see quickly that traditional material was not only handed on but also fitted into a total conception, whose interpretive function should by no means be underestimated. It would also be inadequate to limit the redactional elements exclusively to the external framework and to additions; we know only too well that this interpretation significantly influenced and altered the material itself.[31]

2. What applies to the gospels as we have them applies equally to the material transmitted orally. But here the process of interpretation took place over a longer period, and at the same time was more and more tightly compressed. Sayings and narratives were subjected to reinterpretation more than once, even if on each occasion this may have left its mark in only quite small modifications of the content.[32] So the original meaning was not necessarily lost, but on the other hand it cannot be recovered directly from the present wording. A special kind of problem must also be considered at this point: We have not only the phenomenon of tradition reworked in the interest of new interpretation; we have also the fact that new material was created. In this context let us leave aside the question of how these new creations could be made;[33] what is more important for the present is that the so-called church creations cannot from the outset be distinguished from authentic sayings, because they were handed on indiscriminately as sayings of the Lord. For this very reason they make our access to the preaching of Jesus before Easter considerably more difficult. We need only recall the sharp disagreements between the exegetes as to whether a particular piece of tradition, such as Matt. 16:18f., goes back to Jesus or not in order to point up the fact that this is by no means only a question of details which may or may not belong to the basic stock of his preaching. In this matter, the question of identifying just where new creation takes place soon arises, that is, in which

passages there has been added some new substance, which had no place in Jesus' original message.[34] The total number of completely new creations may not be unduly large, so that what we chiefly encounter is the phenomenon of the recasting of sayings, though admittedly this is in some cases very far-reaching. It cannot be disputed that we have in any case to take account of some such process of revision, and that the Jesus tradition has thereby been overlaid with interpretation in a manner which our scrutiny cannot always immediately penetrate.

3. The decisive point of this process, which alone made possible both the late, redactional alterations and the reinterpretations that took place in the oral tradition through reshaping, additions, or new creations, has to do with the radical transition from the pre-Easter to the post-Easter tradition, which Franz Mussner has called "the process of kerygmatic transformation."[35] For the moment we do not need to argue whether this process of kerygmatic transformation took place all at once, or (what is much more likely) only gradually made itself felt, and therefore emerged in the various branches of tradition with different degrees of intensity. What cannot be disputed is that it arose because of the confession of faith which was inaugurated by the Easter event. But in this respect the gospels already represent an advanced stage of reflection. The older tradition made no distinction at all between the pre-Easter and the post-Easter situation: by contrast, the gospels state emphatically (at least in some passages) that the resurrection of Jesus made possible a new and deeper understanding than the disciples had had before.[36] On the other hand, that does not eliminate the fact that in the New Testament the pre-Easter history of Jesus is almost exclusively viewed and described in the light of the Easter event. In this respect the gospels are not to be distinguished from the older tradition. But that is precisely where our difficulty lies: the pre-Easter tradition lies before us only in the perspective from which it was viewed after Easter. At first glance, this is a considerable source of error. It is in any case an obstacle barring our way, at least at the beginning, in our historical investigation of Jesus. The whole pre-Easter tradition was taken over, extended, and also understood in the light of the resurrection of Jesus and of the new beginning marked by it.[37]

This means, therefore, that the Jesus tradition, insofar as it has been preserved for us, has been modified by the early church's post-Easter preaching, not only in its extent, not only in its form, but also in its interpretation. So we must give due weight to this state of affairs, which is imposed by our sources, before we begin to discuss the possibility and theological relevance of a historical investigation into the pre-Easter Jesus.

Consequences for the Historical Inquiry and for the Problem of Authenticity

In the preceding sections I have deliberately tried to describe the complicated situation confronting us at the outset of our investigation into the pre-Easter Jesus with reference to selection, shaping, and reinterpretation; but I have not gone into details concerning the methods needed for the analysis of the gospels. Of course, this description could be given only because we already have at our disposal fairly dependable results from the work of form and tradition criticism, literary criticism and redaction criticism, and the general and religious history of the New Testament and its world. At the same time, in view of the many kinds of questions that have been debated in recent years, we cannot overlook the fact that these various lines of research must once more be scrutinized and carefully coordinated with respect to the problems to which they are applied, their capacity to resolve those problems, and their demarcation.[38] Their exact differentiation and the ways in which they complement and limit one another play a considerable part in each individual task of exegesis.

But now we must also observe that the historical investigation of the pre-Easter Jesus is a question distinct from all these exegetical steps. No doubt it builds on the results that they produce, and cannot absolutely dispense with analyses of that kind. But it is a methodologically independent procedure, whose individuality needs to be recognized clearly.[39] For here we have to do with a task of historical reconstruction, for which criteria must be established. We must deliberately take a "step back" behind the mass of material handed on by the bearers of tradition, beginning with the first disciples in the time before Easter, so that the figure of Jesus may become visible in its original situation, appearance, and individuality.

The independence of the historical question has important consequences for the much-discussed problem of "authenticity." Since, as we have seen, the Jesus tradition has been modified in its contents, form, and interpretation through its transmission by the post-Easter church, we must begin by assuming that, in a certain sense, the Jesus-tradition is thoroughly "inauthentic." But at this point counterarguments must at once be brought into play. For we can still quite certainly establish that, despite the new understanding that came at Easter, and the process of transformation caused by it, the history of Jesus and Jesus' own words were firmly adhered to.[40] That is true in the fundamental sense that even newly created sayings were identified with Jesus' own words; it is true also with respect to the stock of traditions, since the original Jesus material was the nucleus around which they crystallized. The disciples extended the preaching of Jesus' own message — extended it in a double sense, in that they preserved Jesus' words and deeds, and in that they interpreted his speech and action. Without the basis of the *ipsissima verba* and the *ipsissima facta* that would have been unthinkable.[41] To that extent, "authenticity" is a postulate which cannot be renounced, and which must be investigated concretely in each single case. Nevertheless, in our exegetical work we must not hope to reach conclusions in this respect too quickly. We must be constantly aware of the difficulties involved with reaching back to the pre-Easter Jesus. Yet the alternative, whether the burden of proof lies upon the claim of authenticity or of inauthenticity, is inappropriate.[42] Quite apart from the fact that the historical authenticity or inauthenticity of a passage tells us nothing about the relevance of its contents, the point that really matters is to establish the kind and degree of inauthenticity, that is, of the post-Easter transformation; likewise, on the other hand, it must be shown how the contents of a piece of tradition are related to the preaching of Jesus, and thus what its component of authenticity is. In other words: the relation between pre-Easter and post-Easter elements in the individual pieces of tradition must be examined and precisely defined. Of course, I must begin from the fact that the tradition available to us is that of the early church: but, since the tradition was handed on as a Jesus tradition, I must undertake simultaneously the proof of both authenticity and inauthenticity, because that is the only way in which I can put the distinctive character of this body of tradition into sharp focus.

Conclusions

To end this first part, we must hold fast to four methodologically relevant observations:

1. We must take serious account of the multiplicity of factors which modified the Jesus tradition in the time after Easter: only so shall we have a reasonable prospect of getting through to a complex of tradition that will allow us to draw comparatively reliable conclusions about the preaching, activity, and person of the pre-Easter Jesus. In this sense the search for an "oldest stock" of tradition is justified, though the latter must not immediately be identified with the authentic Jesus tradition.[43]

2. The popular alternative, "genuine saying of the Lord" or "creation by the church," is inadequate for the identification of this oldest stock. Those are only the extreme points of a continuum, and our most pressing task is to provide greater discrimination in the continuum. Only in rare cases shall we find that a "saying of the Lord" has been preserved in a form "genuine" to the last detail. Even when modifying details can be detached fairly easily, our way to the original form in Aramaic remains almost completely barred. Nevertheless, it is likely that some sayings of the Lord were handed on almost unaltered. Likewise, completely new creations are an exception, because what was added by the church in its tradition was closely associated with other transmitted materials, and extended them. All the same, new creations were taken up into the tradition. In the majority of cases we encounter "mixed formations," in which original sayings of the Lord were modified by the setting in which they were placed, extended by additions, or influenced to a lesser or greater degree by reshaping.

3. Usually we shall not succeed in extricating the basic stock by carefully removing later layers, as an archaeologist rescues old material that has been buried. It would be wrong to suppose that we can break through to the pre-Easter Jesus by purely subtractive means.[44] That is why, as we have shown, the question of historical

authenticity or inauthenticity cannot be posed in an alternative but only in a proportional sense. For it is normally not a matter of superimposition, although that does occur too, but of transformation, which cannot summarily be nullified. But this does not exclude the possibility that, in such cases of transformation, particular elements and trends may be discovered which clearly reveal whence alterations of this kind have arisen and whither they are tending — especially if pieces of tradition are compared on a sufficiently broad scale. By doing this, I make it possible to draw inferences about the basis from which such transformations originated. So I must examine further developments in the history of the tradition more closely, so as to be able to identify possible preconditions in the activity of Jesus before Easter.[45]

4. It is only this process of inference from the fixed tradition that makes possible a lively picture of Jesus' activity and person. Only in this way shall we become able to make statements, to use Anton Vögtle's phrase, about the "sense of direction" of Jesus' activity.[46] As we do this, the difference from the tendencies in the post-Easter transmission will come clearly into view: but at the same time a fundamental agreement, too; for without this agreement a Jesus tradition would never have developed among the early Christians. Then it will also become possible to arrange the still ascertainable details of the life of Jesus in their correct order. This means that in our investigation into Jesus we must make more intensive use of an *indirect method*. In this connection Wilhelm Thüsing has proposed that we should search for the *ipsissima intentio Jesu*,[47] that intention which governed his own activity, but which also remained firmly fixed in the tradition, in spite of all the reinterpretation. Because of the distinctive character of the Jesus tradition that has come down to us, I regard this as a correct way of describing the perspective of research.

POSSIBILITIES OF THE INVESTIGATION

We have dealt with the difficulties of the investigation into Jesus: let us now, in this second part, look more closely into the possibilities available to us for reconstructing the activity of Jesus before Easter. For the time being we shall deliberately continue to defer the question of the theological justification of such a procedure; there is more to be done on our historical assignment.

On the Criteria

It is not my task to discuss in detail the criteria by means of which a reconstruction can be undertaken. But it seems to me to be indispensable, in anticipation of the next section, to include at this point in the discussion the consideration of a basic problem. For if we are to make further progress on the methodological problems, beyond the conclusions we have reached so far, we cannot avoid the question of criteria. It is they that permit us to attain results on particular points, and to fit these into a larger context, even if still other paths must be pursued when we attempt a reconstruction, as we shall soon see. Recently there has been a great deal written about the criteria.[49] Surprisingly, however, a comprehensive set of relevant criteria has not yet been achieved. Neither have the possible criteria been adequately collected and arranged, nor has there yet been enough discussion of their soundness.[50] A "criteriology" applied to the historical investigation of Jesus is still awaited.

When one strives after such a criteriology, one should, in my opinion, undertake a differentiation of terminology, so as to facilitate a general view of the problem and to make the criteria usable. For when people speak of "criteria" in current exegetical debate, what is meant in many cases is simply general principles on which the possibility of a historical investigation of Jesus depends, but not specific, individual criteria, which allow a decision with respect to a particular piece of traditional material. Between general principles and criteria properly so-called, a careful distinction should be made. To clarify what has just been said: When Norman Perrin names as criteria the three approaches of dissimilarity, coherence, and multiple attestation,[51] those are indeed important principles, which can bring us for the first time to the authentic Jesus material. Yet they are not criteria in the strict sense. Undoubtedly, these principles have in fact won increasingly greater acceptance;[52] but quite properly there has been talk of other criteria in addition to these.[53]

The following brief remarks can be made about general principles and particular criteria:

1. Sometimes, instead of speaking of the principle of *dissimilarity*, people use the term "critical principle of separation." This means, according to Ernst Käsemann's rule of thumb, that we have comparatively safe ground under our feet only when a tradition can neither be derived from Judaism nor attributed to the early church.[54] Of course, this principle can serve only to define a certain "nucleus" of material as a point of departure; but it breaks down at the point where we have before us undeniable connections between Jesus and Jewish tradition, or, on the other hand, where the early church followed very closely the pattern of Jesus' own manner of expression; and that can definitely be the case, even in statements at the center of the tradition.[55] If we are quite clear about these limitations of its applicability, this principle can certainly be used as a sort of basic clue.

2. The case is rather different with the principle of *coherence*. Recently the term "standard of comparison" [*Gegenkontrolle*] has been used as an alternative, although the two are not fully synonymous. The point is to take individual traditions whose authenticity or inauthenticity is highly probable, compare them with other, similar traditions, and thus draw conclusions about the latter.[56] Conclusions of that kind are permissible only when each group of materials regarded as belonging together presents a fairly consistent picture; but here, again, it must be observed that even material which does not easily "fit" may stand close to the original Jesus tradition, or even belong to it.[57] The question of the coherence both of the reconstructed Jesus tradition and of the various strata of early Christian tradition may perhaps be broadened by means of the principle that, by contrasting them, we can also obtain a "standard of comparison." But in that case we must bear in mind that this can easily produce a false conclusion, since judgments are derived from groupings undertaken by way of experiment, and these judgments by no means do justice to the material.[58]

3. Different again is the case with the principle of *multiple attestation*.[59] It may make inference easier, if elements of tradition which stand close to the authentic Jesus material have not only been handed down in more than one example, but also perhaps reveal

in different contexts an astonishing consistency with respect to form
and content, or else, despite variations, permit us to draw fairly
sound conclusions about the original form. But the decision,
whether what we have is original Jesus tradition, may by no means
be made dependent on the frequency of occurrence; otherwise we
would have to dispense with very important texts for the reconstruction of the pre-Easter activity of Jesus.[60] So this last-named principle can be assigned at most a secondary, confirmative function.

4. Specific, individual *criteria* are a quite different matter. They
may be of a formal character, as for example the use of parabolic
speech or of the introductory *amên*, but they may also have to do
with the contents, such as Jesus' characteristic preaching of the
basileia or his call to discipleship. Halfway between the criteria of
form and of contents comes the use of *abba*. At this very point we
are, surprisingly, still only in the opening stages of working out a
criteriology.[61] Not least among the reasons for this is the fact that
marks of originality, which have been employed in the work of
detailed exegesis, have often been quickly called into question again.
That is shown, for example, by the recent discussion of the word
amên that stands at the beginning of sayings of the Lord.[62] Or it
may be that the criteria to which prominence has been given are
not distinctive characteristics of Jesus alone, but only belong to the
"modes of speech preferred by Jesus," such as the divine passive,
antithetic parallelism, or certain peculiarities of style[63] — not to mention the disputed problem of rhythm in the Aramaic sayings of Jesus.
All the same, if we are to press ahead to reach a broader agreement, much greater progress will have to be made at just this point.
In my opinion that should not be impossible, since there are, with
respect to both form and contents, a whole series of remarkable
indicators which could certainly assume the function of criteria.
Thus it would be worthwhile to see whether, in addition to the
much-discussed parables and parabolic sayings, there may not be
other special features that could be used as evidence: for example,
Jesus' peculiar use of paradox,[64] his use of beatitudes,[65] and, more
generally, his distinctive mode of speech according to which the
present moment of encounter with him corresponds to an event still
lying in the future.[66]

When we employ either the general principles or the particular criteria of form and content, we must, of course, be clear that each of them by itself has, for the most part, only a limited function. It turns out to be the case, over and over again, that observations taken singly fall far short of permitting judgment about a piece of tradition. Individual elements of a formal kind were detachable, and could be used equally well by the church. Characteristic features of content were taken up and reapplied. Only when several criteria are used simultaneously, and when the observations are used to supplement and correct one another, can reliable conclusions be obtained about the assessment of the Jesus tradition for use in the historical investigation of Jesus.

Apart from separating out the oldest stock in the history of the tradition, the general principles and the specific individual criteria have two functions. On the one hand, they are intended to define those traditions which have been transmitted by the early church relatively unchanged or with easily distinguishable additions, and on the other hand, they are to make it possible, by means of an indirect procedure, to draw inferences from traditional material that has been substantially reshaped. That makes sense only if a precise description can be given of those elements which are most probably authentic. That applies not only to the special characteristics of the contents, but also to the formal shaping. The more detailed the results are which can be obtained here, the sooner it will be possible to draw a detailed sketch of the whole picture.[67]

Necessity of a Comprehensive Outline

A reconstruction of the pre-Easter activity of Jesus can be obtained only if a first draft for a comprehensive interpretation is sketched simultaneously with the discovery of detailed pieces of information. Individual observations and an overall view are interrelated at every stage. Now the decisive methodological problem lies in the fact that, when I undertake such a reconstruction, I must enter into a circular argument, whose function, negative as well as positive, must be pondered carefully. For I can make meaningful use of both the general principles and the individual criteria only if I can relate them to a total picture; on the other hand, I am not in a position to obtain a reliable total picture, unless I compose it piece by piece out of detailed observations.

The problem here is not so much how I am to get into this circle, as how I am to keep a continuous check on it. Entry can be obtained fairly easily by trying to obtain, with the aid of the principle of dissimilarity, a first, still very preliminary orientation. I do not need to be afraid of the "minimalizing" tendency of this principle, about which warnings are always being given, if in using it I give heed to this "entry function." Above all, I must at once go on to ask where the decisive clues are to be found for a comprehensive interpretation of the story of Jesus; I am then able to fill in more details of the developing picture, with the aid of individual observations.

Things are more complicated with the control factors that must continue to accompany the process. For I am in danger of supposing that my total picture has already been secured, and of drawing from it conclusions for the analysis of individual problems which are much too far-reaching. Moreover, I must above all constantly bear in mind that I have to work simultaneously with several "total pictures," because this is the only way for me to reach a reliable determination of the relationship between the pre-Easter material about Jesus and that which was handed on and developed in the post-Easter tradition.[68] But these "total pictures" can very quickly come to predominate over the observation of details. In comparison with that task, I have a relatively easy time with the exegesis of the gospels, which were formulated by redaction. For in order to understand the details, I can start with a total framework, which is immediately available to me; and at the same time I can also give an exact description of each individual text with respect to its location and function. Moreover, in the case of Matthew and Luke I have the further possibility of comparison with the Gospel of Mark and with the Sayings source. But when it comes to making judgments about the preaching of Jesus, I must not only begin by contrasting the redactional conceptions of the individual gospels, on the one hand, and a "total picture" of the preaching of Jesus on the other hand; I must also sketch hypothetically a whole series of "total pictures," so as to grasp the distinctive character of the various strands of tradition and the significance of the various centers of tradition.[69] If I wish to avoid getting trapped in a system that will immediately become rigid, these various "total pictures," into which the individual pieces of tradition have to be fitted, must again and again be called into question and reexamined. But if I keep making fresh beginnings with sketches of this kind, which may become very complicated, I shall not get far with working up the material for my purpose. So if I am ever to reach results that can be discussed, involving the total stock of traditional material, I must press ahead to sketch an outline as comprehensive and refined as possible, but which is nevertheless open and flexible enough as to be always capable of revision. The latter can best be done on the basis of precisely those individual observations which could only with difficulty be built into the hypothetical structure that I have used.[70]

Thus, what is needed in order to elaborate a total picture of Jesus' pre-Easter activity is a preliminary sketch, which must constantly be filled out and corrected through the identification of decisive clues and through conclusions reached about individual points. In doing this, it is imperative that one proceed with caution. I may not simply postulate; I cannot hastily fill in gaps for the sake of a total picture that I have imagined. The total picture which is emerging in outline can in the first instance provide me with no more than certain perspectives on the question; it can only indicate to me, as it were, the direction for further search, so that I may locate and evaluate the relevant material. Approaching the question in this way, one must then isolate a particular topic within the overall problem and strive to resolve it by means of an analysis carried out step by step. On this point I refer to Heinz Schürmann's essay, exemplary in its method, on Jesus' understanding of his death.[71] Even if one can agree only in part with its conclusions, one must in any case affirm that its procedure, carried out in minutely detailed steps, is apposite to the subject and remains verifiable at every stage; for this reason, when the question is debated it can immediately become clear where the ways part in the evaluation of the data. But we are still far from having reached the point where all the particular topics have been investigated with such care.

What we have considered in this section has shown that the historical investigation of Jesus can never be isolated methodologically from the examination of the whole history of the tradition until it flows out into the written gospels. In addition, it has become clear that a sketch for the depiction of Jesus' pre-Easter activity constantly needs to be filled out and corrected. In this process, it is just as important to identify decisive clues for the total understanding of Jesus as it is to establish conclusions on points of detail. If there is so close a connection between reconstructing the authentic Jesus material and reconstructing the tradition of the early church, then this means that, with regard to the early church, questions can be asked about its understanding and interpretation of the Jesus tradition and the conditions under which it was transmitted; and on the other hand, with regard to the authentic Jesus material, it must be possible to discover the basis on which the post-Easter tradition was able to be built. For, important as the events of Easter and Pentecost were, the Christian faith cannot be explained exclusively by them. Many significant elements of faith in Christ, of the message about Christ, and of the fellowship of the disciples can be comprehended only through preconditions which lie back in the activity of the pre-Easter Jesus.[72]

Clues for a Total Picture of the Pre-Easter History of Jesus

If we strive to sketch a total picture of Jesus' activity from the methodological perspectives we have just been discussing, we must review the present situation in research. Hitherto the particular criteria of form and contents have been inadequately understood, and only in a few cases do we have studies available which isolate a particular topic step by step. Therefore we can only proceed by holding fast to the basic facts of the history of Jesus which have come to light in exegesis. So as we sketch the outline, which is indispensable for our work, we shall begin from the fundamental "clues" for the understanding of Jesus' activity. These make sense only if they serve to elucidate the phenomenon of Jesus of Nazareth in its totality: that is to say, they must serve as a key, so that the story of Jesus cannot be understood at all without taking them into account.[73] In this way a certain area can be marked out provisionally; of course, it still needs to be examined in closer detail and to be described more precisely. The following sketch will try to clarify the way in which we can undertake a total picture of that kind.

First we must mention two substantial factors of decisive importance: Jesus' conflicts and (to put it in the broadest possible way) the phenomenon of "newness" that was to be perceived when he came on the scene. In both cases there arises the question of Jesus' "impact": on the one hand negatively, as reflected by his opponents, and on the other hand as reflected by those who, to whatever degree, responded to him positively.[74] We shall come across other factors of substantial importance immediately after we have discussed the conflicts and the phenomenon of "newness."

1. It should be undisputed that the *conflicts* are not only highly characteristic of Jesus' public activity but also that they are especially important in opening up extensive insights into his intention.[75] Unfortunately, the passion narrative, which in its various formulations gives expression to the early church's confession of faith, provides us with only limited information about the precise course of Jesus' trial and the charges laid against him.[76] All the same, the reason for which Jesus was condemned can still be discerned. For though it may no longer be possible to bring the early stages of the conflict with the Romans fully to light, it is clear that Jesus was executed as an alleged messianic pretender.[77] It is equally indisputable that the Jews laid charges before the Prefect; but how far this was due to real fears on the part of members of the Sanhedrin about political consequences of the appearance of Jesus is hard to decide. How far, on the Roman side, Jesus' followers were regarded as a threat to public order is a question just as impossible to answer. But at least these questions cannot be summarily dismissed, because Jesus had definitely set in train a certain "popular movement,"[78] even if its character was anything but that of political revolution.[79] In any case, what is decisive is that he was executed for a religious crime.[80]

More important and more instructive for our context are the disputes with the representatives of contemporary Judaism, because they still let us see how things reached that pitch of hostility that finally led to Jesus' death.[81] Disregarding later schematization and narrowing down to "Pharisees and scribes," one may assume from

the material that has been preserved for us that Jesus fell into conflict with the most diverse groups.[82] His activity provoked opposition on the broadest front among the contemporary representatives
of Judaism. And here, no doubt, lies one of the central problems
for understanding the earthly Jesus. Nor can it reasonably be
disputed that this conflict was of basic significance and affected
the foundations of the Jewish faith, especially the understanding
of the Law.[83] Not without reason, the accusation of blasphemy
raised against him runs through the Jesus tradition like a red
thread.[84] For the later church, this accusation was concentrated
on Jesus' messianic claims; but in comparison with the pre-Easter
situation that may be a special sharpening and ultimately a narrow-
ing-down.[85] In the Jewish view a "blasphemer" is a person who does
not submit to the norm of the Law, or, to put it more precisely,
who goes so far as to deliberately transgress the Torah's fundamental
prescriptions, which carry the death penalty.[86] By Jesus' provocative
behavior on the Sabbath, by his disregarding the requirements of
ritual purity, by his attitude toward the sick who were excluded
from society by reason of prescriptions of the Law, it is evident that
he was not prepared to live as a Jew in the Jewish way, in the sense
of the contemporary Jewish self-understanding, no matter of what
shade.[87] That he pronounced to people the forgiveness of their sins,
outside the regular praxis of the cult, and in a controversy could
explicitly take up a position opposed to the Law and the legal traditions, left no room at all for doubt about his nonconformist
behavior.[88]

But now, in all this, Jesus did not merely engage in argument
about the exposition of the Torah of Moses, as was usual among
the various schools of contemporary Judaism. He could obviously
accept post-Old Testament statements, and he could reject them.
For only *one* criterion was decisive for him — whether God's will
is recognized and followed, or whether "human regulations" have
covered over and obscured God's will.[89] But this criterion applied
just as much to the hallowed text of the Law of Moses itself. It is
an oversimplification simply to ask whether Jesus recognized the
Law of the Old Testament or whether he criticized it. Insofar as
God's will can be recognized in it, Jesus of course affirmed the Old
Testament Law; insofar as concessions were made in it to the "hard-

ness of people's hearts," he questioned it.[90] This attitude is only comprehensible if one sees that Moses is no longer the ultimate authority for Jesus. But in the eyes of a pious Jew, faithful to the Law, a person who makes such judgments and behaves in this way is a blasphemer.[91]

2. That brings us at once to the second basic factor. Conflict blazed up over the Law and over the interpretation of the Law; it was a conflict that, despite Jesus' deep commitment to the God of the Old Testament and his revelation in Israel, called into question, at the deepest level, Judaism's self-understanding. Beside this conflict, and in the closest connection with it, the *phenomenon of "newness"* stands as the second key problem for the understanding of the earthly Jesus and the reconstruction of his pre-Easter activity. I am deliberately speaking in a very general way; for it is not enough to say that Jesus claimed to be announcing and putting into effect "something new"; nor is it enough to assert with the benefit of hindsight that "something new" began to happen through him. One must begin with the fact that with Jesus' appearance on the scene there was bound up a real "experience of newness," a quite sweeping awareness, in broad circles of society, of having witnessed the occurrence of something new. Only against that background can we comprehend Jesus' success and also his failure. For it was precisely this "experience of newness" which caused some to assent, but equally provoked others to stiff-necked opposition.

When we ask more precisely what is involved in this phenomenon of "newness," we must, on the basis of the original Jesus tradition that has been preserved, speak of "eschatological newness," which governed his whole activity.[92] It is here that Jesus' attitude toward the Law has its roots, for where God's eschatological revelation comes into effect, even Moses must be measured against it; where the eschatological forgiveness of sins can be received, the ritual ordinances of the Torah are no longer applicable; and where the new order of salvation is constituted, the old order, including even cult and temple, is past, as is unmistakably pointed out by the symbolic action of driving out the traders from the temple.[93]

Jesus' public activity is distinguished by the fact that, in the midst of the world's ongoing life, he proclaims, with his announcement of the *basileia*, the onset of salvation. Thereby he breaks up all traditional patterns of religious thought in Judaism, according to which salvation on the one hand was bound to a sacred past, and on the other hand was reserved for a future in which there was supposed to be a total alteration of the world, or even a completely new world. So the onset of salvation does not mean preliminary signs of salvation, but the realization of this salvation in the present: "Where I by the finger of God am casting out demons, there the kingdom of God has already reached you" (Luke 11:20).[94] Nevertheless, the future salvation remains; it cannot simply be translated into terms belonging to this world, but rather, in an anticipatory way, intervenes in our world from now on, and there leaves behind its tangible effects, even if these are never fully clear to human perception.[95]

At this point, following the usual and correct procedure of exegesis, we must begin with Jesus' parables, for reasons imposed by the history of tradition as well as by the ideas the parables convey. Beside the conflict scenes, the texts that offer our next best possibility of drawing relatively safe inferences are Jesus' parables. Moreover, they are to a high degree distinctive; not only can the parables be clearly set apart in a formal sense from all contemporary analogies, but also by their contents they express in a special way precisely this phenomenon of eschatological newness.[96] In the parables it is made clear that this newness involves a dynamic process, which seeks to lay hold of humankind and the whole world without falling under their control; and that it involves a reality which is still on the way to fulfillment and which is full of promise for the future.[97] Having recognized this, we can make the general assertion that Jesus' preaching is in every aspect characterized by his speaking in parables. Indeed, we can go further: to a large extent his conduct bears parabolic traits.[98] For his actions, too, beginning with his healings and extending through his table fellowship right up to his farewell meal, are meant to be understood as parabolic actions. They are parabolic not in the sense that something is merely supposed to be illustrated by them, but that that reality of eschatological newness, which is already beginning and coming directly upon us, is being made concrete in the present moment and can be experienced right in this world through the signs that Jesus gives.[99]

If in this sense Jesus' miracles, table fellowship, and other deeds are concrete signs of the eschatological Kingdom of God coming into being, then it is not simply the case that for him the life of humankind in this world stands in a relationship to the Last Day, but rather that the light of the Last Day is already shining here. It also follows that decisions which were traditionally reserved for the Last Day are already being made. All that remains for the Last Judgment is to confirm and make public the definitive decisions about salvation and destruction which have already been taken: "Anyone who acknowledges me before men, the Son of Man will also acknowledge before the angels of God; but one who denies me before men will be denied before the angels of God" (Luke 12:8f.).[100]

3. Going a step further, we come across two more basic facts, which however can only be mentioned briefly at this point. Those who declare their allegiance to Jesus are prepared to accept his call to *discipleship*. In the fellowship of Jesus' disciples, all worldly obligations and safeguards are abandoned for the sake of the Kingdom of God, which is now arriving. To become Jesus' disciple is marked both by an unconditional break with one's former way of life and by complete attachment to Jesus' person and work. That is comprehensible only on the basis of the eschatologically new state of things, which attains concrete expression in the life of this human fellowship.[101]

This observation also explains how it is that Jesus lays down new standards of behavior, especially since he gives, as we have seen, only qualified assent to the rules of the Torah. With respect to *Jesus' "ethical" proclamation*, one is again and again surprised at the absence of eschatological motivation.[102] Simply for that reason, it certainly cannot be an "interim ethic."[103] Instead, emphatic reference is made to God's activity as creator. Not only the charge "do not be anxious" but also the command to love one's enemies is motivated by the Creator's providence and kindness. Thus the divine activity in creation becomes the explanation for God's will.[104] But the original will of God, which is affirmed by Jesus over against all tendencies toward casuistry and obfuscation, such as already occur in the Torah of Moses, is now able to be made plain again, for the very reason that the eschatological Kingdom of God is dawning; and from now on the will of God should govern human behavior on this earth in an unrestricted way. Just as the primal time and the end time are connected in Jewish expectation, so here the original will of God is again disclosed in connection with Jesus' message of eschatological newness; and it is brought to expression in such a way that people cannot avoid this claim upon them.[105] This explains both the unconditional nature of the ethical proclamation and its concentration upon love for God and for one's neighbor: and in this setting the command to love one's neighbor demands unlimited application.[106] This corresponds to the fact that when God approaches, bestowing salvation and requiring obedience, there is no longer any intermediate authority or any restriction to a chosen people.[107]

4. Beside Jesus' conflicts and the phenomenon of "newness" which is connected with the dawning of the Kingdom of God, beside discipleship and the articulation of the unrestricted will of God, we come finally upon another circumstance, which serves as a key for understanding the pre-Easter Jesus. We cannot indeed speak in this connection of a "starting point" for the reconstruction of the pre-Easter history of Jesus; it is rather a case of something like a "target point," toward which all our deliberations, even if they remain in many respects incomplete, must find their way — the question of the status and significance of *the person of Jesus*.[108]

It is of substantial importance that the problem be formulated in the right way. It is in my view inadmissible to ask only about Jesus' "self-consciousness" or perhaps even about his "messianic self-consciousness." For on the one hand, the sources yield us virtually no information about Jesus' *self*-consciousness; and on the other hand, "messianic" would have to be defined, and that would require, as a first step, a very precise clarification of what is or is not supposed to be meant by this term.[109] I regard it as equally inappropriate to speak of Jesus' "*consciousness* of mission," because the whole investigation should not be brought onto the psychological plane of "consciousness." But then it is something else if we ask about Jesus' *claim* of mission — the claim, that is, which comes to expression in his preaching, his deeds, and his readiness to accept death.[110]

If we specify the terms of the inquiry in this way, it does not mean at all that we are limiting the field of investigation or excluding certain considerations from the outset, but rather that we need to keep an adequate way of approach to the question wide open.

Because of the nature of our sources, the question of Jesus' claim is extraordinarily difficult and contentious, and it cannot be investigated and answered in detail here. What may however be said is that anyone who draws a connection between the dawn of the eschatologically new state of affairs and his own activity, who because of the eschatologically new state of affairs binds people in discipleship to his own person and takes upon himself a life-and-death conflict about the Torah with the representatives of Judaism, is asserting a claim which cannot be reconciled with the expectations of salvation traditionally held by that Judaism from which he himself springs.[111] Hence it was not for nothing that, because of the history of Jesus, including his death and resurrection, the church in its earliest days saw its chief task to be that of extensively transforming the traditional concepts of salvation, so as to be able to give any account at all of the historical reality that had come about in the person of Jesus.[112]

When anyone puts forward such a claim as Jesus does, it affects the light in which his *whole* life must be seen. Even if we completely disregard God's action in the resurrection as we investigate Jesus in the time before Easter, we must in any case take up the question of what Jesus' death could mean in the light of his activity.[113] For Jesus' appearance on the public scene includes not only the fact that his opponents had him executed because of their conflicts with him, but also the fact that he himself was clearly prepared, right from the outset, to walk the way to the cross. His claim is based on his relation to God. Jesus' behavior implies so unrestricted a relation to God as his Father and as the one who directs his course, that his death cannot be excluded from this association, and so cannot be understood in isolation from this relationship to God.[114]

Conclusions

Two things should have become clear in this second part. First, there are the problems associated with establishing criteria and a comprehensive outline, problems which must accordingly be taken

into account in any attempt at reconstruction. Second, I have sought
to emphasize the specific points from which one must start in seek-
ing to recover a picture of Jesus' history and person which will as
far as possible be faithful and do justice to the time before Easter;
in this regard, as we have seen, his immediate effect on his contemporaries has a special heuristic function. The sketch I have given
needs to be filled out and to be more thoroughly substantiated. But
I wanted to show that research has by now reached the stage at
which, although much work remains to be done, it is already possible to produce, by means of such basic data, a fairly useful total
picture of the history of Jesus.[115]

The failure of the quest of the historical Jesus in the nineteenth
century has led to the recognition, from which we cannot retreat,
that it is impossible to retrace the life of Jesus in the sense of a
modern biography, because to a large extent "biographical" material
is lacking in the tradition. Discussion since then, especially in the
period after the Second World War, has moreover led to the conclusion that one cannot arrive at an understanding of Jesus by means
of a separate investigation either of his preaching or his behavior
or self-consciousness. The task which is still far from accomplished
is that of achieving a detailed and comprehensive elucidation of
the historical person of Jesus and of his appearance in history — an
elucidation which will do full justice not only to the various components of his mission (the proclamation of the dawning Kingdom
of God, the dispute about the Law, the establishment of a fellowship
of disciples, the ethical demand), but also to the various forms of
his behavior and as well to his readiness to take death upon himself
because of the conflict; and which will furthermore enable us to
take up and explain as nearly as possible all the individual details
of the tradition about Jesus that point us back to the history of the
time before Easter.[116]

RELEVANCE OF THE INVESTIGATION

In the first part we were concerned with the difficulties of going
back historically to the pre-Easter history of Jesus, and in the second part we dealt with the possibilities of reconstructing his earthly
activity, but until now we have deferred consideration of the ques-

tion whether there is after all any theological legitimacy in looking for the "historical Jesus." For it is incontestable that the New Testament does not know the pre-Easter Jesus in this sense, and that for many centuries the church's tradition was able to transmit a living faith without needing to pose the historical question in the way we are doing. Only since the time of the Enlightenment has a change come about in this respect. But does the changed way of looking at the question confront the real theological issue? Is there perhaps validity in the thesis which has been proposed and defended, that to go back to the pre-Easter Jesus with the help of modern scientific criticism may be historically important and informative, but essentially pointless, because otherwise faith would have a false basis and moreover would be made dependent on the results of scientific research?[117]

The attempt has been made in various ways to justify the investigation. Yet we must consider very carefully how theologically sound the arguments are which have been offered. It is certainly not enough to say that through the modern development of the history of ideas opportunities have accumulated for us, or have even been imposed upon us, which therefore must also have relevance for our theological efforts, in the interests of intellectual honesty. It is no doubt true that we may not evade the issue here, to the extent that newly posed problems at all events demand an answer of us. But the arrival of modern historical criticism does not in and of itself contain a theologically acceptable legitimation. No, we are confronted with a theological duty only when it can be shown on substantive grounds why I should avail myself of the possibilities of a historical analysis. The task that has newly devolved upon me must therefore be approached and defined in a genuinely theological way. Moreover, that applies not simply to the evaluation of the results of historical investigation; it applies to the whole question of method. For it is only when I can say precisely with what goal and with what presuppositions I am undertaking the establishment of the pre-Easter tradition about Jesus that I can develop an outline of the methods that will be appropriate to the theological task laid down by this project.

Now it should of course be emphasized from the outset that, just as was the case with the generalized affirmation or denial of the possibility of reconstructing the pre-Easter story of Jesus by means of historical research, so it is a false alternative and an inadmissible simplification of the problem to ask whether the historical investigation of Jesus is or is not theologically legitimate. Depending on how the question is posed and pursued, going back to the pre-Easter Jesus can be theologically either inept or in the highest degree legitimate and necessary. In order to make any real progress in this matter, what we must do first of all is mark out carefully the scope of a theologically meaningful inquiry.

Problems of the Historical Investigation

So far we have been approaching the task of reconstructing the history of Jesus without reflection, inasmuch as we have not yet pondered the underlying problems of substantive content. But from the theological point of view the investigation of Jesus is faced with considerable difficulties for this reason, if for no other, that certain grave implications emerge from it which must be critically examined. For it must not be overlooked that preliminary decisions are already involved in the determination of the goal with which the reconstruction of the history of Jesus is being undertaken, and moreover that particular premises are also involved in the historical-critical analysis itself. One must in any case be clear about the reasons for the goal that is set, and the problems inherent in the method of procedure should at least be considered and as far as possible canceled out.

1. If we turn first of all to the *determination of the goal*, we come upon distinctive, basic models which have appeared one after another since the question of the "historical Jesus" first arose in the eighteenth century, and which can still be observed to this day.[118] The demand that one should go back to the "sources," not only in the literary but also in the historical sense, is very much older. It was already playing an important part in humanism and in the period of the Reformation, and helped in the challenging of an overwhelming tradition. In the period of the Enlightenment this demand again became a most lively concern, because the changed mental outlook believed in the possibility of a new approach to the

sources, and therewith a new evaluation of them. To be sure, the principle of going back to the sources did not at first affect the conviction that these sources have immediate significance for the present. Yet at this very point a problem soon emerged, as Lessing clearly showed, in that a certain tension was created between history and relevance to the present, when "accidental truths of history" and "necessary truths of reason" were set over against each other.[119] But that meant, on the one hand, that in the last analysis the question of the "historical Jesus" by no means arose at that time out of a genuinely historical interest, and that on the other hand conformity to reason was the real criterion, which also had to guarantee relevance to the present. That had the effect of raising for the following period the issue of the contingency of historical events and of the function of human reason; and this approach, which measures what is historically contingent by the standard of human reason, has continued to be influential down into our own time. Accordingly, Jesus is understood as the protagonist of human reason, as it becomes successful and gains its autonomy.[120]

Things were different in the nineteenth century. If idealism and romanticism had achieved an intensification of the consciousness of history, positivism caused historical thinking to come into prominence, side by side with the rising natural sciences. For people were trying to find as "objective" a basis as possible for the understanding of humanity and of the world, and were striving to illuminate those facts which could be known and verified with certainty. It is not by chance that what took place then was a systematic development of the historical-critical method. The problems involved in historicism and its understanding of reality came to be recognized only at a fairly late stage. However, one must not overlook the fact that even then basic elements of positivism were maintained, and that this continues to have its effect, especially in confining attention totally to what happens within this world. In the setting of the historical investigation of Jesus this means that his mere humanity is decisive, and he is viewed primarily in the perspective of his own time and its way of thinking.[121]

To overcome the difficulties of an exclusively positivistic conception of what is historical, the existential interpretation strove to give effect to a way of historical thinking that would transcend a mere concern with facts. The aim was to discover, in the "encounter" with events of a bygone time, new possibilities for one's own existence. The chief hope was that in this way the significance of past events for one's own time, which had become problematic in historicism, would be won back. It is interesting that in New Testament studies the existential interpretation began with the earliest Christian kerygma and moved on to the investigation of Jesus only as a second step.[122] The problem is whether the anthropology presupposed in this approach can do full justice to the biblical material.[123]

Quite apart from the existential interpretation, the question is raised more and more frequently whether it is not indispensable, so far as the relevance of the Christian message for the present day is concerned, to pay more concentrated attention to the fact of Jesus' humanity and for that purpose to make use of modern scientific discoveries. What is supposed to be involved here, however, is not the sheer fact of his humanity, but rather the theme *vere homo*, "truly human," of the Christian creed. This implies that Jesus should be taken far more seriously as a human being than has been the case in the past.[124] Here, then, the historical investigation is being set in the framework of the church's tradition, and the attempt is being made to integrate historical research about Jesus into Christology. But we must consider very carefully whether the modern, historical investigation of Jesus can be so simply combined with a traditional concept. To put it another way: Is it after all really the same thing if I ask, from the dogmatic point of view, about the *vere homo*, and, from the point of view of modern research, about the "historical Jesus"? There is obviously need for further clarification at this point.

But in the first place the point is not to let ourselves be deceived about the dogmatic implications in all these models. Since in each case important prior decisions have their effect, we must examine thoroughly the conditions under which the historical investigation of Jesus can appropriately be undertaken.

2. Independent of the dogmatic premises with which the individual researcher goes to work, we must observe that there are

involved in the *historical-critical method* itself, which is indispensable for the analysis of the tradition about Jesus, numerous implications that will affect the conclusions reached. For that very reason it is difficult to say in a few words how we should assess the theological relevance of the historical investigation of Jesus based on this method. But we must sound a warning against any procedure which tries to cut corners.

I do not want to undertake again a detailed discussion of the problems inherent in the historical-critical method: we have explored this in the opening essay of this book.[125] But we must in any case note that historical research about Jesus is a prime example of the fact that with the aid of such a method one can obtain far-reaching and profitable results, but must at the same time pay toll to an ultimately inadequate tendency in this method. Let us simply note the following points: Historical criticism has as such the aim of marking a basic chronological distinction; that is, it not only brings to light the difference between "once upon a time" and "now," but deliberately emphasizes it. For it is in the nature of historical research to illuminate the object of inquiry with light from its own time, a past time from our point of view, and to make it comprehensible for us. Moreover, the historical-critical method tries to explain individual events only from their immediate, causal connections, and excludes more distant points of reference. An alienation of texts and facts arrived at through historical criticism may be useful if it leads us out of the realm of the familiar and sharpens our perceptions; but it can also dominate us to such an extent that any immediate significance for the present time can no longer be detected at all. Albert Schweitzer described the case brilliantly: "A curious thing has happened to research into the life of Jesus. It set out in quest of the historical Jesus, believing that when it had found him it could bring him straight into our time as Teacher and Saviour. It loosed the bands by which for centuries he had been chained to the rocks of ecclesiastical doctrine, and rejoiced when life and movement came into the figure once more, and it could see the historical man Jesus coming to meet it. But he did not stay: he passed by our time and returned to his own."[126] Historical facts, as they have been compiled with the aid of the critical method, have turned into "petrified history."[127]

In contrast with that, the significance for the present time is the really decisive aspect for the New Testament. So in this regard the historical-critical method is running counter to the intention of the texts being studied. This problem has in many cases been disregarded, and therefore a contemporary application has been undertaken in an unreflective way, as the exegetes have quietly slipped in modern categories of understanding and a set of modern questions. With penetrating insight, Albert Schweitzer pointed out that as soon as the "historical Jesus" was set free from the "rocks of ecclesiastical doctrine" he was trapped under the spell of the ideas predominating among the interpreters in each successive period.[128]

Now after the Second World War, especially following Ernst Käsemann's programmatic essay of 1954, there was talk of the "new quest of the historical Jesus," because people supposed that the false trails of earlier theology could be avoided. In the mind of James Robinson, who first popularized the catchword with his book *A New Quest of the Historical Jesus*,[129] and in the mind of many others, there was no doubt that so much had been learned from the theological approach of kerygmatic theology — represented most influentially within New Testament exegesis by Rudolf Bultmann — that the whole question could now be tackled in a more satisfactory way. More satisfactory, because it was assumed that from now on the predominant importance of the kerygma, or at least its indispensable correlation with the question of the historical Jesus, could no longer be disregarded.[130] But it was a serious fallacy when people were presuming, in those days, that the question of the historical Jesus could virtually never again be divorced from this correlation. In many cases today people are speaking of the historical Jesus as if the whole discussion triggered by Bultmann had never taken place; and though the historical investigation of Jesus is being pursued with much interest and intensity, it is in danger of finishing up yet once more in a dead-end street. That is by no means to say that we are absolutely bound to adhere to Bultmann's theological conception; the point is rather that the issue which he perceived and reflected on with absolute clarity cannot be evaded.

3. This brings to light a *crucial problem*, a question which has never yet been adequately thought through: How completely dare one break the characteristic New Testament connection between the history of Jesus and the post-Easter kerygma? Obviously that must be the starting point, if we are to define the terms of the historical investigation of Jesus in a way that does justice to the biblical testimony and is theologically significant. To ask this question neither rules out a serious concern with the church's centuries-old tradition of doctrine, nor does it prejudge the historical effort to get to know the pre-Easter Jesus as inadmissible. By the same token, the earliest Christian kerygma cannot simply be regarded, with all its diversity, as a fixed quantity to be taken over uncritically.[131] But the historical investigation of Jesus will be improperly undertaken if one supposes that the stucco has only to be chipped off the original brickwork by means of the historical-critical method, and that the post-Easter kerygma can thereby be dispensed with. One should notice that when we turn answers into questions, so as to be able to answer them afresh ourselves, the question is not one that has been posed from the beginning.

On the Concept of the "Historical Jesus"

At this point it is advisable to pause a moment and ask whether the current terminology is adequate for formulating the essential problem with the precision required. For when one employs the usual set of terms, this means for the most part that one has already made a particular decision about method.

The term "historical Jesus" has long since become established and widely accepted. Although there are several exact definitions of it, we must observe that it is frequently used in an unclear or decidedly iridescent way. This is clearly evident when people say that the "question of the historical Jesus" is as old as Christianity and that an interest in the "historical Jesus" can already be traced in the earliest Christian tradition.[132] But are statements like that useful and acceptable?

When we speak of the "historical Jesus," what we really mean (to quote the definition from Peter Biehl's research survey) is "Jesus, insofar as he can be made the object of historical-critical study."[133] So this means that when I speak of the "historical Jesus" I am presupposing both the historical consciousness of modern people and the methodological apparatus developed in modern times. That is why Gerhard Ebeling can put it this way: "historical Jesus" is an "abbreviation for: Jesus, as he comes to be known by strictly historical methods, in contrast to any alteration and touching up to which he has been subjected in the traditional Jesus picture."[134] When Ebeling goes on to say that "historical Jesus" means the same as "the true, the real Jesus," then we must add, by way of qualification, that this is true in the sense of the modern understanding of reality. We must begin by recognizing that we are under obligation, if not bondage, to this understanding of reality, and therefore have to obtain our knowledge of history, as of everything else, in this way; and that is what we are doing in exegesis, as much with respect to the earliest Christian kerygma as to the pre-Easter Jesus. But that does not alter the fact that the expression "historical Jesus" does not simply and solely mean the Jesus of history, but includes at the same time a particular way of regarding him.

Nevertheless it does make a difference whether I begin with my modern historical outlook and knowledge and inquire into their possible theological relevance, or whether I simply identify this outlook with that of the Bible. In the latter case I can of course fairly easily derive from the relevance of the Jesus tradition in the New Testament a relevance for my modern quest of the "historical Jesus" also. But it was not without reason that so early a writer as Martin Kähler pleaded for the "historic, biblical Christ" over against the "so-called historical Jesus," thereby emphasizing, over against the modern viewpoint, the unity of history and kerygma in the New Testament witness.[135] Now the discussion about Bultmann's hermeneutic shows how unproductive a distinction between the terms "historisch" and "geschichtlich" is, especially when the term "historisch" is oriented toward historicity as objective facts and "geschichtlich" toward its existential structure, for in both cases modern concepts are involved. "Historical" (*Geschichtlich*) must in my opinion remain a general term, and as a rule that is what it actually is.

But then how can one best describe this matter as it stands in the New Testament? There are several possibilities. When one's attention is directed toward questions about the development of traditions, it makes sense to draw a distinction between the "pre-Easter Jesus" and the "post-Easter congregation." On the other hand, if one has in view the specifically Christological interest of the earliest Christian preaching, then one should speak of the "earthly Jesus" and of Jesus as the "exalted Lord." It is certainly beyond dispute that all the early Christian preaching shows a fundamental interest, albeit of varying extent and in varying expression, in the "earthly Jesus." But it would be a mistake to identify this at once with our search for the "historical Jesus."[136]

But now our problems of terminology also affect the phrase "historical Jesus" itself. Just because it is supposed to take us back to Jesus in his concrete, pre-Easter history, but at the same time gives expression to a particular attitude and approach, the question arises whether this term is a very happy one. Reinhard Slenczka has proposed that we should instead speak of the "historical question about Jesus," and this suggestion should most certainly be taken up in exegetical research.[137] Then we shall avoid speaking of the "historical Jesus" when we mean the earthly Jesus of the early Christian preaching, and we shall at the same time be able to make it clear that we are concerned in different ways with the one and the same Jesus of the time before Easter. We shall then give expression to the unity and the difference between our way of posing the question and that of the earliest Christians, in that we are dealing with the same "object" of consideration but with a mode of "regarding" it which is dependent on modern presuppositions.

In a debate about the problem of the "historical Jesus" Walter Schmithals has rightly emphasized that when we speak of the "historical Jesus" or of the "biblical Christ," what is at issue is a "dogmatic Jesus."[138] He makes this assertion because of the modern premises which are involved in the historical question about Jesus. If we leave aside for the time being the conclusions which he draws, it is important that the term "historical Jesus" should no longer be used or at least should not be used unreflectively. It would be better to give it up altogether, and replace it on the one hand by speaking of the "pre-Easter" or of the "earthly Jesus" and on the other by designating our modern exegetical endeavor as the "historical question about Jesus."

The Earliest Christians' Interest in the History of Jesus

The decisive task with which exegesis is confronted, so far as the historical question about Jesus is concerned, lies in appropriately defining the relationship between the pre-Easter Jesus and the early church's proclamation of Christ. To put it more precisely, we must inquire and demonstrate how it ever came about that Jesus was bound to that "rock of ecclesiastical doctrine," the early Christian kerygma and the later dogma, and what significance there is in this growing together. Precisely at this point, we can expect that important insights will be gained with the help of historical criticism. We would then be able, as the next step, to look for an answer to the question about the theological relevance of the historical question about Jesus.

We must however be clear that in reconstructing the pre-Easter history of Jesus we are carrying out a "step backward," with which the earliest Christians were unfamiliar, and for the good reason that they were concerned not with a step into the past, but rather with the decisive step from the earthly Jesus to the risen Jesus, that is, with the "step forward."

But that does not mean that in the New Testament there was no interest of any kind in the history of Jesus. If the New Testament does not carry out a "step backward" into the pre-Easter situation (to leave aside, at least for the time being, all subsequent events), it is at least familiar with a "glance backward" from the exalted to the earthly Jesus. We must briefly explain the interest in the history of Jesus which is expressed in this way, before we can give an answer to the question of the relevance of our historical endeavors to discover the pre-Easter Jesus.

"The New Testament bears witness to the unity of Jesus and

Christ. It does not separate the Jesus who preaches from the Christ who is preached, but ties the preaching of Jesus Christ to the story of his earthly life. Therefore the history and the preaching of Jesus Christ belong together."[139] That is the leading idea of the new book about Jesus by Heinrich Zimmermann, which accordingly is more a Christology than a historical investigation of Jesus. Let us leave aside the question whether Zimmermann, by this procedure, really does justice to the problems of historical analysis, of which indeed he also makes abundant use in his research into the early Christian kerygma. In any case, he rightly follows the New Testament in taking as his point of departure the early Christian confession and the way in which it ties Christian faith to the person of Jesus.[140]

1. There can be no doubt that in the confession the primary aspect is the presence of the risen and exalted Lord, though that does not mean that the earthly history of Jesus is lost sight of. As we have seen, the distinction between the confessional tradition which predominates in the New Testament epistles and the Jesus tradition proper should not be pressed too hard. Not only have both types of the preaching of Christ a single center,[141] they also have a common interest, which basically consists in holding fast to the *identity* of the earthly and the risen Jesus.[142] So the confessional tradition also has quite specific points of contact with the pre-Easter history of Jesus, which keep turning up regularly: his mission, his incarnation, his death.[143] These points of contact are meant to include his whole earthly existence. The Jesus tradition, on the other hand, has the distinctive character of reporting concrete, specific incidents concerning the earthly Jesus. To that extent, there is a certain truth in saying that the Jesus tradition, in distinction from the confessional tradition, is interested not only in the fact but also in the nature of the earthly history of Jesus; but it likewise does this so as to explain the contemporary significance of this history in the context of the preaching of Christ.[144]

2. Not only the identity but also the *continuity* between the earthly Jesus and the exalted Jesus is important. At this point there has been much unnecessary dispute, because the question of continuity and discontinuity has been discussed in far too broad a fashion. A separate problem, which we took up earlier, is the con-

tinuity of tradition. Without doubt, this continuity exists, but it too was not carried through without interruption. A rather different matter is the continuity in the essential reality. That there is continuity here is of fundamental importance for the testimony given by the New Testament. Of course, the deep rupture caused by Jesus' death is likewise clearly marked. Consequently, what is involved here is not a continuity within the events of this world, but a continuity newly created by God through his action in raising Jesus from the dead, a continuity that is not subject to the conditions of earthly history.[145]

3. In addition to the identity of person and the continuity provided by God's action, the interest of the early Christians in the history of the earthly Jesus is characterized above all by the conviction that the *uniqueness* of this history must be clearly affirmed: it is unique in the sense of being "once and for all."[146] The history of Jesus is the abiding point of reference for Christian preaching and Christian faith. In view of the contingency of Jesus' earthly life, Käsemann is right to speak in this connection of "condescension" and the way the New Testament deliberately affirms that salvation comes from outside ourselves (*extra nos*) and is not subject to our control.[147]

4. All *other aspects* which have been put forward to explain a special interest in the history of Jesus on the part of the earliest Christians are secondary to these three basic motives. This applies to the concern, evident in some passages of the New Testament, to combat enthusiasm and docetism,[148] as also to the increasing use of the Jesus tradition in paraenesis.[149] Virtually all that is happening in these cases is that those basic motives are applied to contemporary problems and for that purpose given additional emphasis. Moreover, what has just been said also holds true over against the claim that a genuinely "historical" interest can already be shown to exist in the New Testament.[150] For on the one hand it is only Luke of whom that can be said with a certain degree of truth, not the other gospels or even the gospel tradition; on the other hand, even Luke's "historical" interest is not directly comparable with our historical thinking and questioning, and so it could fit in with the presuppositions of a confessional outlook to a quite different extent. One

obstructs one's own access to the interest in the history of Jesus within the early Christian tradition, if one works here with our modern ideas and concepts.

All the interest in the earthly Jesus that we encounter in the New Testament, in different varieties, is embedded in the basic concern for confession and preaching. But can we also say anything more particular about the relation between the kerygma and the history of Jesus? The question comes to a head in the problem, which has often been debated in recent discussion, whether and to what extent the history of Jesus could be a substantive criterion for post-Easter preaching.[151] At least it does not perform this function in a one-sided way, such that the early Christian kerygma would have to be measured exclusively against facts of the history of Jesus. But it does perform it, inasmuch as there actually can be no Christian preaching without the "glance backward" to the earthly Jesus. Where people are quite certain (and for early Christianity it was unquestioned) that the decisive factor is the Jesus who is proclaimed as the present Lord, reference to his earthly existence is indispensable. This is so since he is the basis and content of faith precisely because of his history, the significance of which has become apparent in the light of the resurrection.[152]

The Historical Investigation of Jesus in Connection with the Process of Reception in Early Christianity

The observations we have now made allow us to tackle afresh the question of the theological relevance of the historical question about Jesus.

1. In the light of the specific interest in the history of Jesus, which is tied to the kerygma, what is the point of our carrying out the "step backward" and historically reconstructing the pre-Easter activity of Jesus? If this "step backward" is accomplished, then, to judge from the New Testament, it can obviously make sense and be theologically legitimate only if it does not stand alone, but leads back again to that other, forward-moving step, which is directed toward Easter and the abiding presence of salvation.

This means that, as we work our way through a critical analysis, we have to detect how Jesus' own message, which we are reconstructing, was gathered up into the testimony of his disciples and of the early church. At precisely this point, there falls to the historical inquiry about Jesus an eminent duty, whose special significance has until now hardly been seen. For, on the basis of our modern intellectual presuppositions and methods, we are in a position to set out this whole *process of reception* in detail for our inspection.[153] In this way, modern scholarly exegesis is putting us into the position where we can take fresh hold of a genuinely biblical state of affairs. We are no longer restricted to stating the end result, in its different varieties, of this early Christian reception of the Jesus tradition: we are also able to demonstrate in detail how this reception took place. In that case, it ought to be possible for us not only to understand better the answers that were given, but also to discover the original questions underlying them. If the historical investigation of Jesus is approached in this way, then its theological legitimacy can no longer be doubted.

2. If we pose the historical question about Jesus in this manner, several facts which are to be observed in the setting of the pre-Easter history of Jesus can be placed in the comprehensive picture much more easily. For example, it is frequently pointed out that I most certainly do not encounter there a message or a personality that can more easily be transposed or modernized, if I really take Jesus' announcement of salvation and his claim of mission seriously.[154] The call to faith and discipleship is set before me in Jesus' original message (even though it was proclaimed in a situation which for me is in the past) in just the same way as it is in the preaching of the post-Easter period. What the post-Easter Jesus tradition brings to expression, on the other hand, is the enduring relevance to the present time.

Jesus' message itself is also a message about the Kingdom of God *which is breaking in*. It looks forward to the future and the consummation, but at the same time it refers to each new present time. When this forward-pointing function of Jesus' preaching is recognized, one will need to beware of simply historicizing it.[155] But this means that, because of its own specific character, one must never isolate the reconstructed history of Jesus and make it autonomous.

Moreover, Jesus' own history continued. Not only does the "cause of Jesus" continue after his death; his resurrection is part of the whole story, and it may not be cut loose from its relation to his earthly activity.[156] To be sure, the event of Easter is not an immediate object of the historical question about Jesus, but it does affect the process of reception and the early Christian kerygma, which, for its part, I must investigate with the aid of an analysis of the history of tradition, and ask what its basic affirmations are. In doing this, I shall be quite unable to verify historically either the testimony to the resurrection of Jesus or his message of the inbreaking Kingdom of God, since these are matters that directly concern faith. In the context of the early Christian kerygma, one must consider not only the resurrection of Jesus but also the reference to the activity of the Spirit, which was closely linked with Jesus' exaltation. It was not without reason that the early Christian witnesses regarded the events of Easter and Pentecost as confirmation of the continuing realization of the Kingdom of God announced by Jesus.[157] At the same time, in view of these events, it was inevitable for them to make Jesus himself into the decisive content of their preaching.

As we strive to deal with all this in connection with the process of reception, the historical investigation of Jesus must in no way be curtailed; but it will be given an orientation which not only does justice to the New Testament, but also allows many elements in the history of Jesus to be seen more clearly. Wolfgang Trilling has rightly pointed out that there runs through the history of Jesus a "peculiar openness," and this does not remain hidden even in a historical investigation.[158] But it is only in the light of the Easter faith that this openness can be explained, and that is why Trilling can also go on to say that the only "true and clear" Jesus is the Jesus of the kerygma.[159]

Consequences for a Theology of the New Testament

It seems that the matters we have been considering up to this point allow us to tackle afresh and to carry further the discussion, started years ago and never finished, as to whether the reconstruction of the message and history of Jesus constitutes part of a theology of the New Testament, and hence of a Christian theology in general.

As we all know, Rudolf Bultmann stated categorically that the "historical Jesus" does not belong to the theology of the New Testament.[160] In his thesis that the preaching of Jesus belongs simply to the "presuppositions," it must be observed that for him the "kerygma of the earliest church" and the "kerygma of the Hellenistic church before and contemporary with Paul" also fall under the "presuppositions and motifs of New Testament Theology." However, one cannot overlook the real distinction which consists in the fact that, although Jesus' call for decision indeed "implied" a Christology, it was only in the light of the Easter faith that "Jesus' having come" became "itself the decisive event" that established Christian faith and gives it its distinctive character.[161] This means that it too can be a subject of theology, although it is not until Paul and John that we come across a theological concept which has been thoroughly worked out. Yet for Bultmann preceding treatments of Jesus' message have a merely preparatory character.

On the other hand, Joachim Jeremias has always insisted that we must go back to the *ipsissima vox* in the strict, objective sense. For "only the Son of Man and his word can invest our message with full authority."[162] Moreover, the kerygma, the preaching about Christ by the early church, "leads us back from itself at every turn," and "the origins are always to be found in the message of Jesus."[163] So the historical Jesus, as he can be recovered by our research, is the first and essential theme of a theology. Hence Jeremias himself devoted the entire first volume of his *New Testament Theology* to this subject.[164] Apart from his conviction that with the aid of modern research one can attain reliable results,[165] his two main theses are: If we apply ourselves "to the study of the historical Jesus, the final result is always the same: we find ourselves confronted with God himself"; and, "The gospel of Jesus and the kerygma of the early church . . . are related to one another as call and response."[166]

Where interest is directed to a theology of the New Testament as a whole, and the aim is not merely to reduce the perspective to the pre-Easter Jesus, the views of scholars can hardly be more divergent. Without being able to discuss the two proposals in detail, we can say in reply to Jeremias that his scheme of "call and response" does not do justice to the complicated relation between the message of Jesus and the early Christian preaching, for of course the kerygma itself became the decisive "call." Moreover, his statement that we "are confronted with God" touches on one of those distinctive features of Jesus' entry into the world's affairs, which points beyond the specific historical situation of his own history.[167] On the other hand, one can hardly agree with Bultmann, who wants to exclude the preaching of Jesus completely from the theology of the New Testament. Admittedly, an isolated account of the history of Jesus (insofar as we are still in a position to reconstruct it) has no theological relevance; yet one should consider whether within a theology of the New Testament an account should not be given of that very process of reception among the early Christians.

Hans Conzelmann has made an interesting attempt to modify Bultmann's concept. Although he likewise represents the thesis that "the 'historical Jesus' is not a theme of New Testament theology,"[168] he sets out the "synoptic kerygma"[169] in a different way from Bultmann; that is, he undertakes an account of how the Jesus tradition was received in its final stage, through redaction criticism. It must be asked whether his procedure has been sufficiently consistent, for to a large extent this chapter of his corresponds to what Bultmann dealt with under the "presuppositions"; apart from the section devoted to the theology of the synoptists, he here sketches out the main contents of the pre-Easter preaching of Jesus. More important for me is another objection: If one begins by taking up the Jesus tradition in its redactional form in the synoptics, then attention must be paid to the process of reception at all other levels of the early Christian tradition.

The consequence of what we have been saying is that we must deal with the whole transition from the pre-Easter Jesus to the preaching of the early church, and the incorporation of his earthly history into the apostolic testimony; and we must begin with a sketch of the technical problems bound up with the historical investigation of Jesus. Here we must take seriously the fact that depicting the pre-Easter history of Jesus in isolation, however interesting it may be historically, has no theological function on its own. For it is the living, present Christ to whom a commitment is made in faith, and to whom testimony is borne by the earliest Christians; hence it is he that must be made the real point of departure for a theology of the New Testament. That does not do away with the question about the origin of this early Christian message. In order to trace the process by which this reception was carried out, and to reflect on it theologically, we may, indeed we must, pose the historical question about Jesus. But then we do this not simply for the sake of intellectual honesty, because this kind of questioning is forced upon us in our time, but because this is exactly the way in which we can come at the essential problems themselves. So the form of the historical question is not, or at least not exclusively: *What* can I possibly affirm about the pre-Easter Jesus, leaving the post-Easter tradition and history completely out of account? Its form is rather: *How* did the traditions which I can still, for good reasons, identify and lift out as the original material enter into the original preaching, and *why* did that happen?

This marks out a broad field to be worked on in the production of a total theology of the New Testament. But in my opinion it should give us a way of coming out from the aforementioned blind alley in the historical inquiry about Jesus.

Conclusions

"Who is this?" This question, asked by the people when Jesus appeared in public, and by his disciples, has never left people alone since the days of his earthly activity. In our faith and our theological reflection we are again and again confronted by this one decisive question. But we cannot answer it, if we think that we can cut the earthly Jesus loose from his links with the early Christian message.

The attempt to explain the theological relevance of the historical question about Jesus has produced a number of results, which may once more be indicated briefly:

1. In any historical investigation of Jesus, one must understand clearly that there are dogmatic implications involved, and therefore the nature and aim of the investigation must be pondered carefully. The danger of letting oneself be influenced by premises derived from modern intellectual history is great; but the problems of the

historical-critical method itself may not be overlooked either. What is required is to find a genuinely theological way of approach, and as far as possible to avoid the method's immanentist tendency.

2. We have seen that the central problem for a theologically legitimate way of approach is that of determining the relation between the pre-Easter history of Jesus and the post-Easter kerygma. Yet in this regard we must be clear that our historical question about Jesus is not simply identical with the interest of the early Christian preaching in the pre-Easter activity of Jesus. The early Christians were interested not in the "historical" Jesus, Jesus detached from the Easter testimony, but in the "earthly Jesus," in his identity with the risen and exalted Lord. A first consequence of this is that we may not equate the way the early Christians referred to the history of Jesus with our problem, as is done over and over again. Besides, this state of affairs should be reflected in a more precise terminology. For we may not overlook the special character of our historical question about Jesus; and this, in turn, means that we have to make an effort to discover its special function in connection with defining the relation between the pre-Easter Jesus and the post-Easter kerygma. All the same, if we appeal to the identity of the Jesus who preaches with the Jesus who is preached, we certainly do not need to renounce historical investigation.[170] It may be, as Nils Alstrup Dahl has put it, that "faith is *relatively* uninterested in the historical Jesus research," but that does not mean "that it is *absolutely* uninterested in it."[171] It is rather a question of using the historical investigation in order to help illuminate the way the Jesus tradition was received into the kerygma.

3. If this is where the theological relevance of the historical investigation is to be located, then we must go on to explain what real significance there can be in examining the process of reception. The first point to take into account is that the early church could proclaim the abiding presence of salvation in no other way than by giving the message of Jesus a new, Christological interpretation. But it deliberately did not set this new interpretation *alongside* the preaching of Jesus; instead, it reshaped the Jesus tradition. Hence it produced no documentary report on the pre-Easter period, but in essence the procedure it used maintained the identity. It could hold fast to the identity only by interpreting salvation as something

that continued to refer to the present time; and that saved it from being regarded as an episode confined to the earthly life of Jesus. For if the inbreaking of salvation was bound up with the person of Jesus, then everything depended on whether immediate access to this person Jesus was available for every age. After the night of Good Friday, the event of the resurrection made the witnesses certain that this continuing presence of salvation is a reality.

4. But examining how the Jesus tradition was received in early Christianity can also help us (if we see the priority of its application to the present, based on the event of Easter) to explain to what extent the kerygma has "an inner, objectively significant criterion" in the pre-Easter history of Jesus.[172] Though such a "content criticism" is completely justified, it must be handled with the utmost caution. For our historical knowledge may not become the yardstick for the kerygma. We must always look for the essential connection between the kerygma and the history of Jesus; only this relationship can produce that inner criterion which the earthly Jesus must provide for the kerygma. That does not deprive us of the right to probe critically behind the kerygma, but we must begin from the specific starting point of the early Christian preaching as we investigate the history of Jesus as its objective criterion; that is the only way by which to arrive at a true yardstick. This means that in theology we are faced with the task of demonstrating just this inner connection between the pre-Easter Jesus and the post-Easter preaching; only in this setting can the historical investigation be carried out appropriately.[173]

Allow me a few more words by way of conclusion. In the discussion about the pre-Easter Jesus, people have sometimes found it hard to understand that a movement like Christianity could have arisen from a figure such as has been reconstructed by means of historical criticism. Obviously, then, something is wrong with the way in which the text has been handled and the reconstruction done. We have every reason to ponder this.

If I see the matter rightly, four things have an equal place in the task of rediscovering the pre-Easter Jesus: First, detailed academic research, which takes pains with the analysis, arrangement, and evaluation of the traditional material that has been preserved. Then, for the attempt to reconstruct the total picture, there is need for a quality which every good historian should have — an intuitive feel for the greatness of a historical figure and his capacity to change things.[174] Next, for the study of biblical texts there is also need for insight into their genuinely theological way of approaching the question. In making judgments about the pre-Easter activity of Jesus, one needs to recognize the decisive point of reference, and to find an appropriate definition of the relation between the Jesus who preaches and the Jesus who is preached. This is the only way in which the significance of Jesus, which transcends his own time, can be displayed in a fitting manner, which is also valid for our own present age.[175] Finally, the following must also be said in this connection: Ultimately, I cannot understand the pre-Easter Jesus and the early Christian preaching unless I am grasped in faith by this Jesus, who is the Christ and the living Lord. We should have no embarrassment at all about letting this factor play its part at the right place in our scholarly work, without setting limits to the latter's freedom. Theology is a task directed toward faith and having responsibilities to the community of faith. It seeks to arrive, by way of reflection, at an intellectual explanation of its reasons for faith and at a more precise description of Christian existence in the world. Therefore, despite its special premises, it remains an academic discipline, insofar as it gives a clear definition of its relevance to its subject matter. This relevance will be expressed in a specially important way in the struggle to make convincing statements about the continuing significance of the history and person of Jesus for the salvation of humanity and of the world.

NOTES

1. Here, as well as in some later passages, I have incorporated ideas from my guest lecture given in Trier, "Die Frage nach dem historischen Jesus," *TThZ* 82 (1973): 193–205. I call attention also to my 1960 essay, "The Quest of the Historical Jesus and the Special Character of the Sources Available to Us," ET, in Ferdinand Hahn, Wenzel Lohff, and Günther Bornkamm, *What Can We Know about Jesus* (Philadelphia: Fortress Press, 1969), pp. 9–48.

2. A first attempt in this direction was undertaken by Gottfried Schille, "Prolegomena zur Jesusfrage," *ThLZ* 93 (1968): col. 481–88.

3. This opinion, which had often been expressed previously, has recently

been set forth in pregnant form by Georg Strecker, "Die historische und die theologische Problematik der Jesusfrage," *EvTh* 29 (1969): 453-76, esp. 463ff., 468ff. Cf. also Walter Schmithals, "Das Bekenntnis zu Jesus Christus," in *Jesus Christus in der Verkündigung der Kirche* (Neukirchen-Vluyn: Neukirchener Verlag, 1972), pp. 60-79, esp. pp. 75ff.

4. Leaving aside the older research, which presupposed a number of definitive "eyewitnesses" as bearers of tradition, we must mention here especially those interpreters who, despite formal shaping of the tradition by the church community, believe in a firm, basic stock of "historical recollection." Typical is Ludwig Köhler, *Das formgeschichtliche Problem des Neuen Testaments*, Samml. gemeinverständl. Vortr., 127 (Tübingen: J. C. B. Mohr [Paul Siebeck], 1927), pp. 24ff. See also the recent contribution of Rolf Schäfer, *Jesus und der Gottesglaube* (Tübingen: J. C. B. Mohr [Paul Siebeck], 1970), pp. 21ff.

5. An attempt to sketch the fundamental difficulties is undertaken by Francis Gerald Downing, *The Church and Jesus*, SBT, Series 2, no. 10 (Naperville, Ill.: Alec R. Allenson, 1968). However, his work, too, is strongly directed toward the problem of the presuppositions of individual scholars, and is on the whole extremely skeptical with respect to the possibility of reconstructing the pre-Easter activity of Jesus and the oldest history of the church (see, for example, p. 51).

6. See above, pp. 50-64.

7. A typical example of this is the fact that, by comparison with Mark, Matthew has made extensive abridgments in the miracle narratives; on this see Heinz Joachim Held, "Matthew as Interpreter of the Miracle Stories," in Günther Bornkamm, Gerhard Barth, and Heinz Joachim Held, *Tradition and Interpretation in Matthew* (Philadelphia: Westminster Press, 1963), pp. 165-299, esp. pp. 168ff. There is also the well-known omission of Mark 6:45−8:26 in the Gospel of Luke.

8. As an example, we need only mention Matt. 8:18-22/Luke 9:57-62, where we must ask the question whether Luke 9:61f., despite the absence of a parallel, must not be regarded as part of the Q tradition. On this problem, cf. Heinz Schürmann, "Sprachliche Reminiszenzen an abgeänderte oder ausgelassene Bestandteile der Redequelle im Lukas- und Matthäusevangelium," in *Traditionsgeschichtliche Untersuchungen zu den synoptischen Evangelien*, Beiträge (Düsseldorf: Patmos Verlag, 1968), pp. 111-25.

9. In Mark, the most likely place to suspect an omission is where we have an independent, parallel tradition. Thus one may, for example, ask whether Mark 3:22ff. was handed on in tradition without reference to a specific occasion (cf. Luke 11:14 par.). The evangelist could let the latter go, because of his editorial framework. In most cases, however, a judgment is difficult, because variations may go right back to oral tradition.

10. This is clear from a comparison of the traditions of Mark and Q, and in particular from passages where in each case there are different com-

binations of pieces of tradition. Because of the close relationship between the parables of the mustard seed and of the leaven, it is overwhelmingly probable that they were handed on together from a very early stage (Luke 13:18f., 20f./Matt. 13:31f., 33). In Mark, on the other hand, the parable of the mustard seed appears in combination with that of the seed growing by itself, which has a substantially different character (Mark 4:26–29, 30–32); presumably, therefore, in pre-Marcan tradition it had already been taken out of its earlier context.

11. On the problem of the Aramaic substratum of Jesus' sayings, see Matthew Black, *An Aramaic Approach to the Gospels and Acts*, 3rd ed., (Oxford: At the Clarendon Press, 1967); Joachim Jeremias, *New Testament Theology: The Proclamation of Jesus* (New York: Charles Scribner's Sons, 1971), pp. 3ff.

12. See the compilation of Aramaic elements in Jeremias, *New Testament Theology*, vol. 1, 3ff., 35f.

13. On the expression "Easter rift," see Franz Mussner, "Der 'historische' Jesus," in *Jesus in den Evangelien*, ed. Wilhelm Pesch, SBS 45 (Stuttgart: Verlag Katholisches Bibelwerk, 1970), pp. 38–49, esp. pp. 40, 49.

14. Schürmann, "Die vorösterlichen Anfänge der Logientradition," in *Traditionsgeschichtliche Untersuchungen*, pp. 39–65, refers especially to the "sociological continuity" of the circle of disciples and to the authorization given to the disciples to preach, because of which a "continuity of confession" may at the same time be presumed (pp. 47f.).

15. As a rule, the process of selection is not examined in a thoroughgoing manner; all the same, there are references to the problem, e.g. in David Flusser, "Die konsequente Philologie und die Worte Jesu," in *Almanach auf das Jahr 1963*, ed. F. Wittig (Hamburg: F. Wittig, 1963), pp. 39–73, esp. pp. 70f. ("selective character" of the tradition); Schille, "Prolegomena zur Jesusfrage," col. 483 ("process of selection"); Kurt Niederwimmer, *Jesus* (Göttingen: Vandenhoeck & Ruprecht, 1968), p. 23 ("filtering").

16. The Christological "narrowing down" is to be seen most clearly where a kerygmatic tradition has been developed in substantial independence from the detailed traditions of the history of Jesus; often it refers only to his death and resurrection, or else to his mission or incarnation. Yet the two branches of tradition may not be distinguished in principle, as has again been done recently by Siegfried Schulz, "Die neue Frage nach dem historischen Jesus," in *Neues Testament und Geschichte: Festschrift für Oscar Cullmann*, ed. Heinrich Baltensweiler and Bo Reicke (Zürich: Theologischer Verlag Zürich; Tübingen: J. C. B. Mohr [Paul Siebeck], 1972), pp. 33–42, esp. pp. 36ff. The "kerygma tradition" may have remained largely independent, but it has in any case exercised a strong influence on the "life of Jesus tradition"; see my remarks in "Methodenprobleme einer Christologie des Neuen Testaments," *VF* 15 (1970): esp. 32ff.

17. To these belong especially the proclamation of the Kingdom of God, the call to discipleship, the shared meals, the encounter with opponents, the miraculous deeds, and the history of the passion and resurrection. To that extent, the changed situation after Easter also provided the very circumstances which made it possible for the tradition to be taken over and carried further. Moreover, we can see from this that what is involved in the selection is not only a general phenomenon of the handing-on of traditions (such an objection has been raised by Rudolf Pesch); rather, the handing-on of the Jesus tradition is subject to quite particular external and internal conditions which need to be defined and taken into account.

18. Let me simply mention texts like Luke 12:49f.; Matt. 11:12f. (par.); Mark 9:49f.

19. Deliberate collection obviously began much earlier in the case of the sayings than of the narrative materials. It can be seen in Mark that the sayings material is either combined in small collections or attached to narratives (e.g. Mark 11:23–25; 2:21f.); on the other hand, narratives were taken over by the evangelist in part one by one and in part in groups (e.g. Mark 1:40–44; 4:35 – 5:43).

20. See the basic works on form criticism, especially Martin Dibelius, *From Tradition to Gospel* (1919; ET, New York: Charles Scribner's Sons, 1935), pp. 1ff.

21. Along these lines, Rudolf Bultmann, *The History of the Synoptic Tradition* (1921; ET, New York: Harper & Row, 1963) began by thoroughly investigating the changes in traditions, along with determining their forms.

22. See Schürmann, "Die Sprache des Christus," In *Traditionsgeschichtliche Untersuchungen*, pp. 83–108.

23. "Style" means here not just an external, linguistic attribute, but the whole mode of presentation and putting things into words; see Dibelius, *From Tradition to Gospel*, p. 7.

24. See e.g. Mark 9:43, 45, 47f. with Matt. 5:29, 30 (special material), which leads one to suspect that Mark 9:45 is an additional formation by analogy. Something similar can be observed by comparing Luke 12:2f/Matt.10:26f. with Mark 4:22.

25. This can be demonstrated from the various strata of translation in the Septuagint as well as from Philo's exposition of Scripture.

26. On this problem, see Joachim Jeremias, *The Parables of Jesus*, rev. ed. (New York: Charles Scribner's Sons, 1963), pp. 20f; Matthew Black, "The Recovery of the Language of Jesus," *NTS* 3 (1956–57): 305–13; Hans Peter Rüger, "Das Problem der Sprache Jesu," *ZNW* 59 (1968): 113–22.

27. However, we are not to suppose in this regard that Jesus himself instructed the disciples with a view to the preservation and transmission of the tradition in the manner of the Rabbis; so Harold Riesenfeld, *The Gospel Tradition and Its Beginnings* (London: A. R. Mowbray, 1957). Rich comparative material from the rabbinic tradition is offered by Birger

Gerhardsson, *Memory and Manuscript*, ASNU 22 (Lund: C. W. K. Gleerup; Copenhagen: Einar Munksgaard, 1061); see also *Tradition and Transmission in Early Christianity*, ConNT 20 (Lund: C. W. K. Gleerup; Copenhagen: Einar Munksgaard, 1964). See the work of Schürmann mentioned in n. 14; also Etienne Trocmé, *Jesus and His Contemporaries* (London: SCM Press, 1973), esp. pp. 27ff.

28. That is true, for example, of the Sayings source, which does not actually refer to Jesus' death and resurrection, but does have in Matt. 11:27/Luke 10:22 a definite Christological center which would make no sense if it did not in fact imply Jesus' resurrection and his living presence; its closeness to the tradition used in Matt. 28:18-20 is also unmistakable.

29. See, for example, the attempt at a retranslation of the Lord's Prayer in Jeremias, *New Testament Theology*, vol. 1, pp. 193ff.

30. To name a striking example, let me mention Matt. 17:24-29 (the temple tax). Of the sayings, one may recall the "call of the Savior," Matt. 11:28-30 (attached to the sayings about authority, Matt. 11:25-27/Luke 10:21f.), to which there are typical parallels in Jewish wisdom; see Hans Dieter Betz, "The Logion of the Easy Yoke and of Rest (Matt. 11:28-30)," *JBL* 86 (1967): 10-24.

31. In this respect, research into the redaction of the gospels has produced substantial discoveries, even if the redaction-critical approach has at times been carried too far, so that the particular character of the traditional material was no longer adequately seen. See Joachim Rohde's review of research, *Rediscovering the Teaching of the Evangelists* (Philadelphia: Westminster Press, 1968).

32. Thus see Mark 2:21f. in the context of 2:18-20, on which see my essay "Die Bildworte vom neuen Flicken und vom jungen Wein," *EvTh* 31 (1971): 357-75, esp. 369ff.

33. Apart from new creations made by the editors, which are connected with the leading ideas of the gospels, and apart from additions which are to be explained by the process in which traditional materials were collected and arranged, we are particularly concerned here with sayings which, because of their contents, are hard to associate with Jesus' preaching, particularly in cases where they presuppose a distinct Christological concept, or otherwise clearly reflect the situation after Easter. These new creations have often been assigned to early Christian prophets, who spoke in the name of the exalted Lord; but this has again been disputed recently; at least, the discussion has not been concluded. See Fritz Neugebauer, "Geistsprüche und Jesuslogien," *ZNW* 53 (1962): 218-28.

34. See my essay "Die Petrusverheissung Matt. 16:18f. Eine exegetische Skizze," *Materialdienst des konfessionskundlichen Instituts Bensheim* 21 (1970): 8-13.

35. Franz Mussner, *Die johanneische Sehweise*, QuDisp 28 (Freiburg im Breisgau: Herder Verlag, 1965), p. 80.

36. See Mark 9:9ff. par.; especially John 2:22; 12:16 and the Johannine farewell discourses.

37. This will be taken up in more detail above, pp. 65ff.

38. See the criticism (which in part at least is not wholly justified) by Erhardt Güttgemanns, *Offene Fragen zur Formgeschichte des Evangeliums*, BEvTh 54 (Munich: Chr. Kaiser Verlag, 1970); Wolfgang Richter, *Exegese als Literatur-wissenschaft* (Göttingen: Vandenhoeck & Ruprecht, 1971).

39. This was already clearly emphasized by Martin Dibelius, "Zur Formgeschichte der Evangelien," *ThR* n.s. 1 (1929): 185–216. "At this point we stand at the limits of research into historical facts. For form-critical work does not, of course, have the last word in the matter of content criticism; it only has the task of laying the basis, in a methodical and appropriate manner, and as far as possible without the help of subjective guesswork, for ultimate deliberations on matters of content." For here we "enter a field which lies outside the form-critical task" (p. 214).

40. An exception is to be found only in the rules for ordinary conduct, in which sayings of Jesus are handed on without reference to their origin; so e.g. Rom. 12:14; James 5:12.

41. The concept *ipsissima facta* has led to a debate between Franz Mussner and Rudolf Pesch. See Mussner, *Die Wunder Jesu* (Munich: Kösel Verlag, 1967), pp. 33ff.; Pesch, *Jesu ureigene Taten?*, QuDisp 52 (Freiburg im Breisgau: Herder Verlag, 1970), esp. pp. 15ff., 135ff.; Mussner, "Ipsissima Facta Jesu?" *TRev* 68 (1972): col. 177–84; Pesch, "Zur theologischen Bedeutung der 'Machttaten' Jesu," *ThQ* 152 (1972): 203–13. Without going into the discussion in detail, one can say that the term *ipsissima facta* is useful, if the distinction is maintained between an action of Jesus before Easter and the report about it (see Mussner, "Ipsissima Facta Jesu?" col. 181 with n.8).

42. That authenticity must be proven has recently been asserted once again by Norman Perrin, *Rediscovering the Teaching of Jesus* (New York: Harper & Row, 1967), p. 39. Jeremias, *New Testament Theology*, vol. 1, on the contrary, demands: "In the synoptic tradition it is the inauthenticity, and not the authenticity, of the sayings of Jesus that must be demonstrated" (p. 37).

43. This oldest stock can only serve to mark out those elements which are in any case more recent, even if there should still be reflected in them something characteristic of Jesus. Thus what must be done is to identify the material that is of primary importance for getting back to the pre-Easter Jesus.

44. This is rightly emphasized by Christoph Burchard, "Jesus," in *Der kleine Pauly*, vol. 2 (Stuttgart: Alfred Druckenmüller Verlag, 1967), col. 1344–54, esp. 1345f.: the Jesus tradition becomes a source for the pre-Easter Jesus through a "reduction" to what is original, "which can no longer be

carried out through subtraction." Schille, "Prolegomena zur Jesusfrage," col. 486: "Our material is not appropriate for the method of peeling off layers. It is kerygma, but not the encapsulated *ipsissima vox et actio* of Jesus."

45. Perrin, *Rediscovering the Teaching of Jesus*, p. 32, is rather too one-sided in requiring that "only the earliest and most original form of a saying" ought to be of interest to us. Werner Georg Kümmel, *The Theology of the New Testament according to Its Major Witnesses: Jesus, Paul, John* (Nashville: Abingdon Press, 1973), insists that it is imperative to reach back for the oldest material, but that in addition the further development must be taken into account as a constant check on the correctness of any isolation of the earliest stock of tradition (p. 26). Especially important is Nils Alstrup Dahl's essay, "The Problem of the Historical Jesus," in *The Crucified Messiah* (Minneapolis: Augsburg Publishing House, 1974), pp. 48–89: The question, how far "it is at all possible to give a scientifically founded and tenable description of the life of Jesus" (p. 49), is in his opinion only to be resolved if the critical study of the gospels sets itself the goal "to make clear the history of the tradition about Jesus within the church" (p. 66). A precise separation between genuine words of Jesus and constructions of the community can in no case be achieved; but through "cross sections," which bring to the fore what was characteristic of Jesus, a "critically assured minimum" can indeed be obtained, just as, on the other hand, a "maximum" must be set forth by drawing, at the same time, "longitudinal lines leading from Judaism beyond to primitive Christianity," for the tradition can be regarded in its totality as "a reflex of Jesus' activity" (pp. 67f., 71).

In similar manner, Harald Riesenfeld, "Bemerkungen zur Frage des Selbstbewusstseins Jesu," in *Der historische Jesus und der kerygmatische Christus*, ed. Helmut Ristow and Karl Matthiae (Berlin: Evangelische Verlagsanstalt, 1960), pp. 331–41, esp. p. 339, calls for a "stereoscopic consideration" of the available sources instead of a method of mere reduction.

46. Anton Vögtle, "Jesus von Nazareth," in *Ökumenische Kirchengeschichte*, vol. 1, ed. R. Kottje and B. Möller (Mainz: Matthias Grünewald Verlag; Munich: Chr. Kaiser Verlag, 1970), pp. 3–24, esp. p. 23.

47. Wilhelm Thüsing, "Neutestamentliche Zugangswege zu einer tranzendentaldialogischen Christologie," in Karl Rahner and Wilhelm Thüsing, *Christologie — systematisch und exegetisch*, QuDisp 55 (Freiburg im Breisgau: Herder Verlag, 1972), pp. 79–305, esp. pp. 182ff. He too opposes the process of subtraction and calls for a combination of methods in the historical investigation of Jesus; it is a matter of detecting "the field of function and relation, which is arranged in a manner that ultimately cannot be confused," in which Jesus is seen within the tradition. In doing

this, he wishes to ask about the *ipsissima intentio* of Jesus, because this term is clearer and more comprehensive than that of the *ipsissima vox*.

48. This means that we may go in search of "historical authenticity" in more than the formal sense. Of course we cannot simply switch over to "authenticity of substance," because in that case the Jesus tradition of early Christianity would have to be taken into account in its totality; rather, we must strive to reach back with the aid of historical indicators, but in a way that is not confined to the essentially authentic sayings and parables and those facts of Jesus' life which are ascertainable with relative certainty. Thus we need a definition of "historical authenticity" which begins with the essential facts of the situation.

49. A survey is provided by Werner Georg Kümmel, "Jesusforschung seit 1950," *ThR* n.s. 31 (1965/66): 15–46, esp. 42ff,; Gerd Theissen and Philipp Vielhauer, *Ergänzungsheft zu Bultmanns Geschichte der synoptischen Tradition*, 4th ed. (Göttingen: Vandenhoeck & Ruprecht, 1971), pp. 10ff.; especially by Martin Lehmann, *Synoptische Quellenanalyse und die Frage nach dem historischen Jesus*, BZNW 38 (Berlin: Walter de Gruyter & Co., 1970), pp. 163ff.

50. Indicative of this is the sharp criticism of the use of fixed criteria in Robert Stewart Barbour, *Traditio-Historical Criticism of the Gospels: Some Comments on Current Methods* (London: SPCK, 1972); see also Downing, *Church and Jesus*, pp. 93ff.

51. Perrin, *Rediscovering the Teaching of Jesus*, pp. 38ff.

52. See Harvey K. McArthur, "Basic Issues: A Survey of Recent Gospel Research," in *In Search of the Historical Jesus*, ed. Harvey K. McArthur (New York: Charles Scribner's Sons, 1969), pp. 139–44; D. G. A. Calvert, "An Examination of the Criteria for Distinguishing the Authentic Words of Jesus," *NTS* 18 (1971–72): 209–19. In the center of the discussion remains Frederick C. Grant, "The Authenticity of Jesus' Sayings," in *Neutestamentliche Studien für Rudolf Bultmann*, BZNW 21 (Berlin: Alfred Töpelmann, 1954), pp. 137–43. See also Franz Mussner, "Der historische Jesus und der Christus des Glaubens," in *Praesentia Salutis*, Gesammelte Studien (Düsseldorf: Patmos Verlag, 1967), pp. 42–66, esp. pp. 44ff.

53. See pp. 53, 54, above, and see also Martin Lehmann, *Synoptische Quellenanalyse*, pp. 189ff.

54. Ernst Käsemann, "The Problem of the Historical Jesus" (1953), in *Essays on New Testament Themes*, SBT 41 (Naperville, Ill: Alec R. Allenson, 1964; reprint ed., Philadelphia: Fortress Press, 1982), pp. 15–47: "In only one case do we have more or less safe ground under our feet; when there are no grounds either for deriving a tradition from Judaism or for ascribing it to primitive Christianity, and especially when Jewish Christianity has mitigated or modified the received tradition, as having found it too bold for its taste" (p. 37). Similarly Hans Conzelman, "Jesus Christus,"

in *RGG*, 3rd ed. (Tübingen: J. C. B. Mohr [Paul Siebeck], 1959), III, col. 619–53: esp. 623 (ET, Philadelphia: Fortress Press, 1973, p. 16): "For reconstructing the teaching, the fundamental methodological principle is to regard as genuine that which belongs neither in Jewish thought nor in the ideas of the later church."

55. Burchard, "Jesus," col. 1346, rightly warns that merely a "bare, minimalistic differential picture" is left. On the difficulties of applying this method, see Martin Lehmann, *Synoptische Quellenanalyse*, pp. 178ff.

56. See Perrin, *Rediscovering the Teaching of Jesus*, pp. 43ff.

57. In this connection the argument is also used that there was something "characteristic of Jesus" or that "he had a typical way of acting"; so Dahl, "The Historical Jesus," p. 67; Burchard, "Jesus," col. 1346; Athanasius Polag, "Historische Bemerkungen zum Leben Jesu," *Lebendiges Zeugnis* 3 (1971): 33–46, esp. 34. Mussner, "Der historische Jesus," p. 45, speaks of the particular, unique "character," which could not be an invention. All that is true enough; but it must be handled with caution, since otherwise it easily leads to false judgments in the isolation of authentic elements of tradition.

58. We shall come back to this when we discuss the need for a "total picture"; see above, pp. 54–57.

59. See Perrin, *Rediscovering the Teaching of Jesus*, pp. 45ff., following Thomas Walter Manson, *The Teaching of Jesus*, 2nd ed. (Cambridge: At the University Press, 1935), pp. 10f.; McArthur, "Basic Issues," pp. 139ff.

60. One needs only to recall the special material of Matthew or Luke; but Marcan tradition too is often handed on several times because of direct dependence on Mark, without occurring again in an independent stream of tradition, such as the Sayings source. See Perrin, *Rediscovering the Teaching of Jesus*, p. 48.

61. Apart from Gustav Dalman, *The Words of Jesus* (Edinburgh: T. & T. Clark, 1909), *passim*, we must on this question depend substantially on the studies of Joachim Jeremias, "Characteristics of the *ipsissima vox Jesu*" (1954), in *The Prayers of Jesus*, SBT series 2, 6 (Naperville, Ill.: Alec R. Allenson, 1967), pp. 108–15; *The Parables of Jesus* (especially worthy of note is the list of "negative criteria," i.e. of the laws of transformation, pp. 113f.); *New Testament Theology*, vol. 1, pp. 36f. By contrast, Käsemann, "The Problem of the Historical Jesus," p. 35, takes the view that, apart from the parables, we possess "absolutely no kind of formal criteria by which we can identify the authentic Jesus material."

62. See Klaus Berger, *Die Amen-Worte Jesu*, BZNW 39 (Berlin: Walter de Gruyter & Co., 1970); "Zur Geschichte der Einleitungsformel 'Amen, ich sage euch,'" *ZNW* 63 (1972): 45–75. See also Victor Hasler, *Amen* (Zürich and Stuttgart: Gotthelf Verlag, 1969). However, neither of these authors has succeeded in the aim of totally disqualifying this criterion.

63. So Jeremias, *New Testament Theology*, vol. 1, p. 9. Apart from

Jeremias, ground has been broken on this field only by Charles F. Burney, *The Poetry of Our Lord* (Oxford: At the Clarendon Press, 1925); Karl Georg Kuhn, *Achtzehngebet und Vaterunser und der Reim*, WUNT 1 (Tübingen: J. C. B. Mohr [Paul Siebeck], 1950); also Black, *Aramaic Approach*, passim.

64. See e.g. Mark 10:25 parr.; 11:23 parr.

65. See Luke 10:23f./Matt. 13:16f.; Luke 6:20f./Matt. 5:3, 4, 6.

66. Typical of this is the structure of Luke 12:8f.

67. Even if the approach toward illuminating the *ipsissima intentio* of Jesus is predominantly indirect, we shall not be able to give up the attempt to establish the greatest possible number of distinctive, individual elements for the total picture of Jesus, elements that not only convey a "general" impression of his preaching and activity but also bring to light special features of his speech and action.

68. Reference has been made several times recently to the inevitable connection between the identification of the authentic Jesus material and the history of the tradition in early Christianity as a whole; so Schille, "Prolegomena zur Jesusfrage," col. 481ff.; Burchard, "Jesus," col. 1346; Wolfgang Trilling, "Geschichte und Ergebnisse der historisch-kritischen Jesusforschung," in *Jesus von Nazareth*, ed. Franz Josef Schierse (Mainz: Matthias-Grünewald Verlag, 1972), pp. 187–213, esp. pp. 190f. The apocryphal tradition, too, must be taken into account here.

69. Here one must be on guard against oversimplification. It is not enough to set up a distinction between a Palestinian and a Hellenistic branch of the early church, nor is it possible to work with a scheme of "six spheres of tradition or of church life," as is proposed by Schulz, "Die neue Frage," pp. 34f., because although we can name a list of centers of tradition, which have left their mark on a considerable part of the material, we can by no means apportion the whole of the matter preserved in the New Testament to clearly identifiable strands of tradition and centers of tradition.

70. This is true not only of elements which possibly go back to Jesus but which are hard to fit into the picture we have obtained; it is just as true of components which at the outset cannot be accommodated within early Christian tradition.

71. Heinz Schürmann, "Wie hat Jesus seinen Tod bestanden und verstanden? Eine methodenkritische Besinnung," in *Orientierung an Jesus. Festschrift für J. Schmid* (Freiburg im Breisgau: Herder Verlag, 1973), pp. 325–63.

72. See above, pp. 65–80.

73. Along these lines, Rudolf Bultmann, *Theology of the New Testament*, vol. 1 (New York: Charles Scribner's Sons, 1951), pp. 1ff., tried to comprehend the message of Jesus by means of his eschatological message, his interpretation of God's demand, and his idea of God; but a historical

investigation of Jesus is certainly not entitled to confine itself to his preaching. Ernst Fuchs' question about Jesus' behavior is fundamentally justified at this point: *Studies of the Historical Jesus*, SBT 42 (Naperville, Ill.: Alec R. Allenson, 1964), esp. chaps. 1 and 7.

74. At the same time there comes into view, even if only secondarily, the perspective of the "aftereffect" of the history of Jesus in the early Christian period; but we must not for the moment let it become dominant, since we are concerned with an attempt at reconstruction, which should as far as possible be uninfluenced by the post-Easter church's outlook and judgment.

75. This is rightly pointed out with emphasis by Niederwimmer, *Jesus*, pp. 31, 53ff.; in this respect I can only concur with his presentation, though I am quite unable to accept his remarks about Jesus' mythical mode of speech and picture of God (pp. 37ff., 66, 69f.).

76. See Josef Blinzler, *Der Prozess Jesu*, 4th ed. (Regensburg: Pustet Verlag, 1969); Paul Winter, *On the Trial of Jesus*, Studia Judaica 1 (Berlin: Walter de Gruyter, 1961); David Catchpole, *The Trial of Jesus*, Studia Post-Biblica 18 (Leiden: E. J. Brill, 1971).

77. Despite Bultmann's misgivings, the historicity of the inscription on the cross is not to be called into question; I refer to my remarks in *The Titles of Jesus in Christology* (Cleveland: World Publishing Co., 1969), pp. 160f. With good reason Dahl, *The Crucified Messiah*, pp. 10–36, emphasizes that it was precisely Jesus' death as a messianic pretender that gave a decisive impulse to the understanding of his activity within the post-Easter church.

78. See Martin Dibelius, *Jesus* (Philadelphia: Westminster Press, 1949), chap. 4.

79. See Martin Hengel, *Was Jesus a Revolutionist?*, Facet Books, Biblical Series 28 (Philadelphia: Fortress Press, 1971); Oscar Cullmann, *Jesus and the Revolutionaries* (New York: Harper & Row, 1970); Erich Grässer, "'Der politisch gekreuzigte Messias.' Kritische Anmerkungen zu einer politischen Hermeneutik des Evangeliums," in *Text und Situation*. Gesammelte Aufsätze (Gütersloh: Gerd Mohn, 1973), pp. 302–30.

80. This fact must not be overlooked, even if the charge against him was politically motivated, or the Roman Prefect understood it that way.

81. From this perspective the question may also be raised, how far "failure" was characteristic of Jesus' activity; see Polag, "Historische Bemerkungen," pp. 39f. However, on the basis of the material available I am not convinced that we should think in terms of a formal "crisis" due to increasing failure; so again recently Franz Mussner, "Gab es eine 'galiläische Krise'?" in *Orientierung an Jesus*, pp. 238–52.

82. This designation of the opponents has become general in the Gospel of Matthew, but the same tendency is also discernible in Mark. A different perspective is still to be seen clearly in Mark 12:18–27 parr.

83. See Käsemann, "The Problem of the Historical Jesus," pp. 37ff., and Günther Bornkamm, *Jesus of Nazareth* (New York: Harper & Brothers, 1960), pp. 96ff.

84. See Mark 2:7 parr.; 14:64 parr.; John 10:33.

85. This is shown especially in the narrative of Jesus' confession before the High Council in Mark 14:55–65 parr.

86. The deliberate breach of the Sabbath belongs here, in any case; see Exod. 31:14f.; 35:2; also Num. 15:32–36.

87. See Mark 2:23–28 parr.; Mark 7:15 par.; Mark 1:40–44 parr.; Mark 2:14–17 parr., to mention just these.

88. So Mark 2:5ff. parr.; Luke 7:47; Mark 10:1–12 par. No doubt these texts in their present form have all been shaped by post-Easter transformations, but they still enable us to draw inferences about Jesus' behavior.

89. See Mark 7:8 par.; what was said in the previous note holds true likewise for the dispute in Mark 7:1–13 par.

90. See Mark 10:5 par.

91. A different view is taken by Klaus Berger, *Die Gesetzesauslegung Jesu*, vol. 1, WMANT 40 (Neukirchen-Vluyn: Neukirchener Verlag, 1972), see esp. pp. 576ff. I am not at all convinced that the basic thesis put forward in this book is right. See the more recent work of Hans Hübner, *Das Gesetz in der synoptischen Tradition* (Witten: Luther Verlag, 1973), esp. pp. 226ff.

92. This is expressed most clearly in his proclamation of the *basileia tou theou*.

93. See Mark 11:15–17 parr.; John 2:13–22. A constant element in all the texts is the key expression "to drive out" (*ekballein*), and so one should also speak of the "driving out from the temple" (*Tempelaustreibung*). Where sacrificial animals are chased away and it is made impossible to change the money needed for sacrificial gifts, a regular cult can no longer be carried out. However, a reinterpretation in the sense of a "cleansing of the temple" and its use as a "house of prayer" is already beginning in early Christian tradition, as Mark 11:16, 17a shows.

94. In the parallel passage Matt. 12:28, the figurative use of "finger of God" is replaced secondarily by "spirit of God."

95. Hence the demand for signs, Mark 8:11f. parr.

96. The copious literature on the parables cannot be discussed here. On the basic question let me simply refer to Bornkamm, *Jesus of Nazareth*, pp. 64ff.; Eberhard Jüngel, *Paulus und Jesus*, 4th ed., Herm. Unters. z. Theol. 2 (Tübingen: J. C. B. Mohr [Paul Siebeck], 1972), pp. 87ff.

97. See Nils Alstrup Dahl, "The Parables of Growth," *StTh* 5 (1951–52): 132–66, but see also Jeremias, *Parables of Jesus*, pp. 146ff., who especially emphasizes the contrast.

98. See Jüngel, *Paulus und Jesus*, pp. 135ff. However, Strecker, "Problematik der Jesusfrage," pp. 462f., rightly calls for a "correlation of the

parabolic stories with the whole of Jesus' preaching," since otherwise there is the danger that these texts will be interpreted in too narrow a way.

99. Gustav Stählin, "Die Gleichnishandlungen Jesu," in *Kosmos und Sympathie. Festschrift für Wilhelm Stählin* (Kassel: Joh. Stauda Verlag, 1953), pp. 9–22; Heinz Schürmann, "Die Symbolhandlungen Jesu als eschatalogische Erfüllungszeichen. Eine Rückfrage nach dem historischen Jesus," *Bibel und Leben* 11 (1970): 29–41, 73–78.

100. I refer to my exposition in *Titles of Jesus in Christology*, pp. 26f., 29ff.

101. See my essay, "Pre-Easter Discipleship," in Ferdinand Hahn, August Strobel, and Eduard Schweizer, *The Beginnings of the Church in the New Testament* (Minneapolis: Augsburg Publishing House, 1970), pp. 9–39.

102. This problem is mentioned by Hans Conzelmann, "Zur Methode der Leben-Jesu-Forschung," *ZThK* 56 (1959): Beiheft 1, pp. 2–13, esp. pp. 11ff.; "Jesus Christus," *RGG*, 3rd ed., III, col. 637ff. ET, *Jesus* (Philadelphia: Fortress Press, 1973), pp. 59ff.

103. Against Albert Schweitzer, *The Quest of the Historical Jesus* (New York: Macmillan Co., 1968), pp. 354, 366, and passim.

104. See Matt. 5:44–47 for just one example.

105. Against the sharp separation in Conzelmann, "Zur Methode der Leben-Jesu-Forschung," p. 12, who sees a link only in the hearers' immediate confrontation with God in each case. But a case is to be made for a closer substantive connection with eschatology; see Anton Vögtle, "'Theo-logie' und 'Eschato-logie' in der Verkündigung Jesu?" in *Neues Testament und Kirche. Festschrift für Rudolf Schnackenburg* (Freiburg im Breisgau: Herder Verlag, 1974), pp. 371–98.

106. See Mark 12:28–34/Matt. 22:35–40/Luke 10:25–28; also Luke 10:29–37.

107. Where the original will of God becomes the criterion for human behavior, the Law can no longer be an intermediate authority in the Jewish sense. That Jesus in his pre-Easter activity concentrated on the people of Israel is not to be denied; but his message had a universal tendency, and for that reason it is not by chance that a crossing of the boundaries of Israel is probable right from the time of Jesus' activity, though that does not mean that he already carried out a "gentile mission" in the strict sense. See my comments in *Mission in the New Testament*, SBT 47 (Naperville, Ill.: Alec F. Allenson, 1965), pp. 26ff.; in addition, Martin Hengel, "Die Ursprünge der christlichen Mission," NTS 18 (1971–72): 15–38, esp. 35ff.

108. It is impossible to discuss the immense literature here. For an outline of the problem see Bornkamm, *Jesus of Nazareth*, pp. 169ff., and in addition the literature in n. 110 below. Besides, it must be remembered that the problem of the status and significance of the person of Jesus is of course also raised even in interpretations which think only in terms of an "im-

plicit Christology" (so especially R. Bultmann, *Theology of the New Testament*, vol. 1, pp. 42ff., Conzelmann, "Jesus Christus," *RGG*, 3rd ed., III, col. 650f.; ET, pp. 88ff.), even if in that case it has its effect on the account of the pre-Easter history of Jesus in a different way.

109. In the Jewish sense it cannot of course be used at all, no matter which variety of Jewish expectation one starts from. Moreover, the relation between "Messiah" and "Son of Man" would first have to be defined precisely, since this was a matter of the utmost tension in the Judaism of that time, and still represented a considerable problem for post-Easter Christology as well. The assertion that the life of Jesus was "unmessianic" is at first sight a question of terminology; but behind it there lies hidden the problem of specifying exactly what concepts there were in Judaism and early Christianity concerning the bringer of salvation. The alternative, "either apocalyptic-messianic or unapocalyptic-unmessianic," in August Strobel, *Die moderne Jesusforschung*, Calwer Hefte 83 (Stuttgart: Calwer Verlag, 1966), pp. 43f., is of no use. See on the other hand the interesting reflections on the subject by Franz Mussner, "Der 'historische' Jesus," pp. 69–80, esp. pp. 74ff.

110. Instead of the "claim of mission" one could also speak of the "claim of authority"; occasionally, too, the expression "claim of faith" is used, but that leads in a rather different direction. The detailed description of the claim of mission must, of course, be drawn from what can be gained with some certainty from the authentic Jesus material. See Werner Georg Kümmel, "Der persönliche Anspruch Jesu und der Christusglaube der Urgemeinde" (1963), in *Heilsgeschehen und Geschichte*, Gesammelte Aufsätze (Marburg: N.-G. Elwert Verlag, 1966), pp. 429–38; Norbert Brox, "Das messianische Selbstbewusstsein des historischen Jesus," in *Vom Messias zum Christus*, ed. Kurt Schubert (Vienna: Herder Verlag, 1964), pp. 165–201, esp. pp. 185ff.; Franz Mussner, "Wege zum Selbstbewusstsein Jesu," *BZ* n.s. 12 (1968): 161–72; Eduard Schweizer, *Jesus* (Richmond: John Knox Press, 1971), pp. 13ff.; Joachim Gnilka, *Jesus Christus nach frühen Zeugnissen des Glaubens* (Munich: Kösel Verlag, 1970), pp. 159ff.; also Anton Vögtle, "Exegetische Erwägungen über das Wissen und Selbstbewusstsein Jesu" (1962), in *Das Evangelium und die Evangelien. Beiträge zur Evangelienforschung* (Düsseldorf: Patmos Verlag, 1971), pp. 296–344; Martin Hengel, *The Charismatic Leader and His Followers* (New York: Crossroad, 1981), pp. 63ff., 69f. The discussion of the problem in Jeremias, *New Testament Theology*, vol. 1, pp. 250ff., remains problematic, because here post-Easter tradition is too strongly drawn on for Jesus' own consciousness of special dignity.

111. It is no doubt more appropriate to describe this claim of Jesus in some detail than to set it into a relation of partial agreement or divergence with traditional models of expectation; early Christianity saw itself as already confronted with this task, and so it substantially reshaped the inherited concepts of the bringer of salvation.

112. See my study, *The Titles of Jesus in Christology*; also Reginald H. Fuller, *The Foundations of New Testament Christology* (New York: Charles Scribner's Sons, 1965), esp. pp. 102ff., 142ff.; Rudolf Schnackenburg, "Christologie des Neuen Testaments," in *Mysterium Salutis*, ed. Johannes Feiner and Magnus Löhrer (Einsiedeln: Benziger Verlag, 1970), III//1, pp. 227–388.

113. I refer to the works of Schürmann and Dahl mentioned in n. 71 and n. 77.

114. On the relationship to God, see Wilhelm Thüsing, "Das Gottesbild des Neuen Testaments," in *Die Frage nach Gott*, ed. Joseph Ratzinger, QuDisp 56 (Freiburg im Breisgau: Herder Verlag, 1972), pp. 59–86, esp. 77ff.

115. The best available account of the pre-Easter history of Jesus is that of Bornkamm, *Jesus of Nazareth*.

116. In attempting this comprehensive view, not only may one begin from the assumption that a relatively unified concept underwent a development into complex forms, but at the same time one must also bear in mind that a very complex state of affairs could to some extent disintegrate and become simplified in the post-Easter period; see Schille, "Prolegomena zur Jesusfrage," cols. 483, 485. This means, therefore, that for reasons of method I must presume that there was a complicated body of data both within the preaching of Jesus and within the preaching of the early church, and that I can discover particular relationships only after painstaking research on individual questions. See Werner Georg Kümmel, "Diakritik zwischen Jesus und dem Christusbild der Urkirche," in *Heilsgeschehen und Geschichte*, pp. 382–91.

117. See e.g. Rudolf Bultmann, "Das Verhältnis der urchristlichen Christusbotschaft zum historischen Jesus" (1960), *Exegetica* (Tübingen: J. C. B. Mohr [Paul Siebeck], 1967), pp. 445–69, esp. pp. 450ff.

118. On this point, I refer to the important book of Reinhard Slenczka, *Geschichtlichkeit und Person Jesu Christi*, Forsch. z. syst. u. ökum. Theol. 18 (Göttingen: Vandenhoeck & Ruprecht, 1967), esp. parts 1 and 2, where, with particular regard to the Jesus research of the eighteenth and nineteenth centuries, the question of dogmatic presuppositions is discussed in detail.

119. See the essay "On the Proof of the Spirit and of Power" (1771), in *Lessing's Theological Writings*, ed. Henry Chadwick (London: A. & C. Black, 1956), pp. 51–56.

120. See Albert Schweitzer, *The Quest of the Historical Jesus* (New York: Macmillan Co., 1968), pp. 27ff. Correspondingly, Niederwimmer, *Jesus*, p. 7, can call biblical criticism "an activity of critical reason."

121. Typical of this attitude, for example, is Herbert Braun, *Jesus of Nazareth: The Man and His Time* (Philadelphia: Fortress Press, 1979), pp. 1–2, where it is asserted: "Jesus the true human being is the clear foun-

dation of the New Testament. . . . If Jesus was an actual human being, then he lived at a particular time and in a particular environment. . . . That is why we ask, 'Who *was* Jesus of Nazareth?'" See Peter Stuhlmacher, "Kritische Marginalien zum gegenwärtigen Stand der Frage nach *Jesus*," *Fides et Communicatio. Festschrift für Martin Doerne* (Göttingen: Vandenhoeck & Ruprecht, 1970), pp. 341–61, esp. pp. 350ff., 360ff. On the other side, it must not be forgotten that it is precisely to systematic historical criticism that we owe such discoveries as that of the peculiar character of Jesus' eschatology; see Johannes Weiss, *Jesus' Proclamation of the Kingdom of God* (German original 1892; ET Philadelphia: Fortress Press, 1971).

122. This is true on the one hand of the numerous publications of Rudolf Bultmann, and on the other hand of the works of Ernst Fuchs, *Studies of the Historical Jesus* (Naperville, Ill.: Alec R. Allenson, 1964) and *Jesus. Wort und Tat* (Tübingen: J. C. B. Mohr [Paul Siebeck], 1971); Gerhard Ebeling, *Word and Faith* (Philadelphia: Fortress Press, 1963), esp. pp. 201–46, 288–304. Here too belongs James M. Robinson, *A New Quest of the Historical Jesus*, SBT 25 (Naperville, Ill.: Alec R. Allenson, 1959).

123. Yet it should not be overlooked that the theologians named have made a decisive contribution to the discussion of the historical question about Jesus. Above all, they have faced up to the problem of the theological justification of the historical investigation of Jesus. I do not have the opportunity here for a detailed evaluation and criticism.

124. See e.g. Josef Blank, *Jesus von Nazareth. Geschichte und Relevanz* (Freiburg im Breisgau: Herder Verlag, 1972), pp. 5ff., 13f.; though the "historical Jesus" and the "Christ of faith" cannot be separated, the human person Jesus is of "extreme interest." Schäfer, *Jesus und der Gottesglaube*, laments the absence of a "picture of Jesus produced by historical research and recognized everywhere" and says, "But today, without a picture of the historical Jesus there can scarcely any longer be a Christology" (p. 111).

125. See above pp. 13–33.

126. Schweitzer, *Quest of the Historical Jesus*, p. 399. See above, p. 33, n. 18.

127. Käsemann, "Problem of the Historical Jesus," p. 24.

128. Schweitzer, *Quest of the Historical Jesus*, pp. 400ff. Schweitzer's book, which first appeared in 1906, has been called the funeral song over research on the life of Jesus; but meanwhile a second volume could be written, which would be at least as thick. In place of the pictures of Jesus as the optimistic enlightener, the sober rationalist, the romantic in union with nature, the fiery eschatological fanatic, there would come forth today the pictures of Jesus as the critic of society, the social reformer, the campaigner against oppression, slavery, and exploitation, and the revolutionary.

129. See above, n. 122.

130. Soon after the first appearance of Robinson's book, the question

was thrown back skeptically, whether what was offered was in fact a new approach; see Van A. Harvey and Shubert M. Ogden, "How Now Is the 'New Quest of the Historical Jesus'?" in *The Historical Jesus and the Kerygmatic Christ: Essays on the New Quest of the Historical Jesus*, ed. Carl E. Braaten and Roy A. Harrisville (Nashville: Abingdon Press, 1964), pp. 197–242. On the American discussion see Perrin, *Rediscovering the Teaching of Jesus*, pp. 230–33; Howard Clark Kee, *Jesus in History*, 2nd ed. (New York: Harcourt Brace Jovanovich, 1977), esp. 293ff.; John Reumann, *Jesus in the Church's Gospels: Modern Scholarship and the Earliest Sources* (Philadelphia: Fortress Press, 1970); Leander E. Keck, *A Future for the Historical Jesus* (Nashville: Abingdon Press, 1971; Philadelphia: Fortress Press, 1982). For English research, see Charles Frances Digby Moule, *The Phenomenon of the New Testament*, SBT, II/1 (Naperville, Ill.: Alec R. Allenson, 1967), pp. 43ff., 56ff.; Charles Harold Dodd, *The Founder of Christianity* (London: William Collins Sons, 1971; New York: Macmillan Co., 1970); Christopher Francis Evans, "Is 'the Jesus of History' Important?" in *Is "Holy Scripture" Christian?* (London: SCM Press, 1971), pp. 51–63, esp. pp. 57ff.

131. One should however be wary of the claim that the unity of the diverse testimony of the post-Easter period is brought to light by getting back behind the texts of the New Testament to Jesus. This is indeed true in the fundamental sense, since the early Christian testimony has its center in the person of Jesus, but it is not true in the sense that this unity could be set forth simply through the historical investigation of the pre-Easter Jesus. See Wolfhart Pannenberg, *Jesus – God and Man* (Philadelphia: Westminster Press, 1968), pp. 21ff.

132. See e.g. Franz Mussner, "Christologische Homologese und evangelische Vita Jesu," *Zur Frühgeschichte der Christologie*, ed. Bernhard Welte QuDisp 51 (Freiburg im Breisgau: Herder Verlag, 1970), pp. 59–73, esp. p. 66.

133. Peter Biehl, "Zur Frage nach dem historischen Jesus," *ThR* n.s. 24 (1956–57): 54–76, esp. 55.

134. Gerhard Ebeling, "The Question of the Historical Jesus and the Problem of Christology," in *Word and Faith*, p. 290.

135. Martin Kähler, *The So-Called Historical Jesus and the Historic, Biblical Christ* (German original 1892; ET Philadelphia: Fortress Press, 1964). *Translator's note*: "By *historisch* Bultmann means that which can be established by the historian's criticism of the past; by *geschichtlich* he means that which, although occurring in past history, has a vital existential reference to our life today," according to Reginald H. Fuller, *Kerygma and Myth*, vol. 1, ed. Hans Werner Bartsch (London: SPCK, 1953), p. xii.

136. The correlative terms "historical Jesus" and "kerygmatic Christ" are, by the way, exegetically useless, at least if what they are supposed to clarify is not the contemporary issues of Christology but the New Testament's outlook. For what the New Testament is concerned with is neither

the contrast of the "historical" and the "kerygmatic" nor an opposition of "Jesus" and "Christ," but rather the assertion that the earthly Jesus is at the same time the Jesus who is proclaimed as Christ. Strictly considered, the "kerygmatic Christ" in this correlation is a mythical figure. One should be just as cautious, too, about setting the "Christ of faith" over against the "historical Jesus," because this does not sufficiently express the presupposed identity between the Christ who is the object of faith and the earthly Jesus. See Gerhard Delling, "Der 'historische Jesus' und der 'kerygmatische Christus,'" in *Studien zum Neuen Testament und zum hellenistischen Judentum*, Gesammelte Aufsätze 1950–1968 (Göttingen: Vandenhoeck & Ruprecht, 1970), pp. 176–202.

137. Slenczka, *Geschichtlichkeit*, pp. 22ff., 138ff.

138. Walter Schmithals, "Antwort an Theodor Lorenzmeier," in *Jesus Christus in der Verkündigung der Kirche*, Gesammelte Aufsätze (Neukirchen and Vluyn: Neukirchener Verlag, 1972), pp. 80–90, esp. p. 82.

139. Heinrich Zimmermann, *Jesus Christus. Geschichte und Verkündigung* (Stuttgart: Verlag Katholisches Bibelwerk, 1973), p. 9.

140. Ibid., pp. 100ff.

141. Ibid., pp. 70ff.

142. See above, pp. 39–40, 44–47, and 49–50.

143. See e.g. Gal. 4:4; Rom. 1:3f.; Rom. 3:24–26.

144. See Ernst Käsemann, "Blind Alleys in the 'Jesus of History' Controversy," in *New Testament Questions of Today* (Philadelphia: Fortress Press, 1969), pp. 23–65, esp. pp. 43ff.; Eduard Schweizer, "Die Frage nach dem historischen Jesus," *EvTh* 24 (1964): 403–19, esp. 410ff., 417ff.

145. On this problem, let me refer to Käsemann, "Blind Alleys," pp. 39f.; Ebeling, "The Question of the Historical Jesus," pp. 298ff.; Perrin, *Rediscovering the Teaching of Jesus*, pp. 242–48; also Ernst Heitsch, "Die Aporie des historischen Jesus als Problem theologischer Hermeneutik," *ZThk* 53 (1956): 192–210, esp. 196ff., 202ff.

146. See Bornkamm, *Jesus of Nazareth*, pp. 22f.

147. Käsemann, "The Problem of the Historical Jesus," pp. 30ff.

148. Käsemann, "Blind Alleys," pp. 47ff., 52.

149. Dibelius, *From Tradition to Gospel*, pp. 233ff.

150. See Hans Conzelmann's 1960 book, *The Theology of St. Luke* (Philadelphia: Fortress Press, 1982) pp. 12 ff.; Georg Strecker, *Der Weg der Gerechtigkeit. Untersuchungen zur Theologie des Matthäus*, FRLANT 82, 3rd ed. (Göttingen: Vandenhoeck & Ruprecht, 1971); "Problematik der Jesusfrage," pp. 472ff.; Rolf Walker, *Die Heilsgeschichte im ersten Evangelium*, FRLANT 91 (Göttingen: Vandenhoeck & Ruprecht, 1967), pp. 145ff.; Jürgen Roloff, "Das Markusevangelium als Geschichtsdarstellung," *EvTh* 29 (1969): 73–93; *Das Kerygma und der irdische Jesus. Historische Motive in den Jesus-Erzählungen der Evangelien* (Göttingen: Vandenhoeck & Ruprecht, 1970), pp. 40ff., 47f. In this last-named book, historicizing is described as "a factor which right from the beginning had

a significant influence on the formation of tradition"; see my comments on this in "Methodenprobleme einer Christologie des Neuen Testament," *VF* 15, 2 (1970): esp. p. 8, n. 14.

151. See e.g. Karl Kertelge, "Der geschichtliche Jesus und das Christusbekenntnis der Gemeinde," *Bibel und Leben* 13 (1972): 77–88, esp. 81: the church's faith in Christ needs "objective criticism, i.e., it must be demonstrated, right through the stereotyped forms in which faith is expressed, that it receives its orientation from the facts of the history of Jesus"; however, it is at the same time affirmed that we may not separate "the question, who Jesus *was*, from the other, who Jesus (for us) *is*."

152. See Gerhard Ebeling, *The Nature of Faith* (Philadelphia: Fortress Press, 1961), pp. 58ff., 72ff.

153. I have already referred to the need for this approach in *VF* 15, 2 (1970): 8f.; also in *TThZ* 82 (1973): 202ff.

154. See Robinson, *A New Quest*, pp. 108ff.

155. The problem of the near expectation and delay of the parousia should not be overrated in this connection. See Erich Grässer, *Die Naherwartung Jesu*, SBS 61 (Stuttgart: Katholisches Bibelwerk Verlag, 1973), esp. pp. 123f., 138f.

156. Franz Mussner, "Die 'Sache Jesu'," in *Catholica* 25 (1971): 81–89, is of course right in saying that there is also a "cause of Jesus Christ" after Easter; but it must be asked whether one should extend that problematic expression in such a way at all.

157. See 1 Cor. 15:20ff.; Acts 2:22ff., 32ff.

158. Wolfgang Trilling, *Fragen zur Geschichtlichkeit Jesu* (Düsseldorf: Patmos Verlag, 1966), pp. 161ff., 164ff.; Trilling says that this openness points positively to "a secret" and that this central secret is the person of Jesus himself. Also Leonhard Goppelt, "Der verborgene Messias," *Christologie und Ethik*, aufsätze zum Neuen Testament (Göttingen: Vandenhoeck & Ruprecht, 1968), pp. 11–26, speaks in this connection of the secret within the history of Jesus; but he tries to anchor it in Jesus' self-consciousness, and thereby asks too much of the sources.

159. Trilling, *Fragen zur Geschichtlichkeit Jesu*, p. 18.

160. Bultmann, *Theology of the New Testament*, vol. 1, pp. 1ff.

161. Ibid., pp. 42f.

162. So already in Jeremias, *Parables of Jesus* (1954), p.7; repeated in the second edition (1963), p. 9. It must be observed that in his meaning the phrase *ipsissima vox Jesu* not only signifies historical originality but also is the essential criterion for all Christian preaching and theology.

163. Joachim Jeremias, *The Problem of the Historical Jesus*, Facet Books, BS 13 (Philadelphia: Fortress Press, 1964), pp. 13, 14.

164. Jeremias, *New Testament Theology*, vol. 1. Since in this work the author does not go into the theoretical issues, the essay mentioned in n. 163 must necessarily be taken into account too.

165. Jeremias, *Problem of the Historical Jesus*, pp. 15ff. Also pp. 14f.: "The Incarnation implies that the story of Jesus is not only a possible subject for historical research, study and criticism, but demands all of these."

166. Ibid., pp. 21, 23.

167. See Käsemann, "Blind Alleys," pp. 24ff.

168. Hans Conzelmann, *An Outline of the Theology of the New Testament* (New York: Harper & Row, 1969), p. xvii.

169. Ibid., pp. 95ff.

170. Against Zimmermann, *Jesus Christus*, p. 9 and passim.

171. Dahl, "The Problem of the Historical Jesus," p. 77.

172. Blank, *Jesus of Nazareth*, p. 6 holds that reference back to the person of Jesus is constitutive for the early Christian understanding of tradition. All the same, I have reservations about the way Blank says that there is a "theologically authentic concern" to get hold of reliable information "about the historical presuppositions of Christian faith" (p. 5), because the reference to the past here can easily be understood in a false sense, as offering historical underpinning for faith. There have of course been efforts of that kind in both Protestant and Catholic circles. On the Protestant side, it was above all the endeavor to set forth the objectivity of the "facts of salvation"; see the summary and criticism in Friedrich Gogarten, *Entmythologisierung und Kirche*, 4th ed. (Stuttgart: Vorwerk Verlag, 1966), pp. 34ff. On the Catholic side, we can point to the form of fundamental theology developed around the end of the nineteenth century; see J. Schmitz, "Die Fundamentaltheologie im 20. Jahrhundert," *Bilanz der Theologie*, vol. 2, 2nd ed., ed. Herbert Vorgrimler and Robert Vander-Gucht (Freiburg im Breisgau: Herder Verlag, 1970), pp. 197–245, esp. pp. 200ff.

173. See the concluding part of Slenczka's book, *Geschichtlichkeit*, pp. 303ff.; in this context he discusses the question of Jesus Christ's being as a person and the personal continuity.

174. On reading many a book about Jesus, one cannot help asking how a picture of Jesus, allegedly rediscovered by strict historical methods, but in fact derived from modern presuppositions, fits in with the presuppositions of thought and understanding of those times; i.e., whether a Jesus who preaches and behaves like that can have been comprehensible at all to people of the first century. This question must be raised with respect to the portrayal of Jesus by Braun, among others.

175. This is the only way to fulfill the expectation that the historical investigation of Jesus will help us through to a new concept of Christology, so that we can gain a fresh understanding of the old ecclesiastical dogmas, which are hard for people of our time to repeat. See the sketch by Walter Kaspar, in *Neues Glaubensbuch. Der gemeinsame christliche Glaube*, 9th ed., ed. Johannes Feiner and Lukas Vischer (Freiburg: Herder Verlag; Zürich: Theologischer Verlag, 1973), pp. 276ff.

SCRIPTURE INDEX

AUTHOR INDEX